LONDON IN MY TIME

By

Thomas Burke

1934

Copyright © 2013 Read Books Ltd.
This book is copyright and may not be
reproduced or copied in any way without
the express permission of the publisher in writing

British Library Cataloguing-in-Publication Data
A catalogue record for this book is available from the
British Library

Thomas Burke

Thomas Burke was born in Clapham, London in 1886. His father died when he was very young, and at the age of ten he was removed to a home for middle-class boys who were "respectably descended but without adequate means to their support." Burke published his first piece of writing – a short story entitled 'The Bellamy Diamonds' – in 1901, when he was just fifteen. However, proper recognition came in 1916, with the publication of *Limehouse Nights,* a collection of melodramatic short stories set amongst the immigrant population of London's Chinatown. *Limehouse Nights* was serialized in three British periodicals, *The English Review*, *Colour* and *The New Witness,* and received positive attention from reviewers and a number of authors, including H. G. Wells. It also sparked something of a controversy, however, and was initially banned by libraries due to the scandalous interracial relationships it portrayed between Chinese men and white women.

It was these portrayals of London's Chinatown that Burke is best-remembered for. However, there is some degree of confusion over how much of Burke's writing was based in fact; as literary critic Anne Witchard states, most of what we know about Burke's life is based on works that "purport to be autobiographical, yet contain far more invention than truth." Whatever the truth, there is no doubt that, in his day, Burke was regarded as the foremost chronicler of London's Chinatown at the turn-of-the-century. Burke told newspaper journalists that he had "sat at the feet of Chinese philosophers who kept opium dens to learn from the lips that could frame only broken English, the secrets, good and evil, of the mysterious East," and these journalists almost uniformly took him at his word.

Burke continued to use descriptions of urban London life as a focus of his writing throughout his life. Off the back of *Limehouse Nights,* Burke published the thematically similar *Twinkletoes* in 1918, and *More Limehouse Nights* in 1921. However, he was a prolific author who tried his hand at a number of different genres. He semi-regularly published essays on the London environment, including pieces such as 'The Real East End' and 'London in My Times', and during the thirties even tried his hand at horror fiction. Indeed, in 1949, shortly after his death, Burke's short story 'The Hands of Ottermole' was voted the best mystery of all time by critics. Burke also influenced the burgeoning film industry in Hollywood; D W Griffith, for example, used the short story 'The Chink and the Child' from *Limehouse Nights* (1917) as basis for his silent movie, *Broken Blossoms* (1919), and Charlie Chaplin derived 'A Dog's Life' (1918) from the same book.

CONTENTS

Spirit of Change .... Page 7

People .... Page 36

Shops .... Page 72

War .... Page 94

Entertainment .... Page 113

Streets .... Page 171

SPIRIT OF CHANGE

Diamond Jubilee. . . . Sixty Years a Queen. . . . The Longest Reign. . . . The roofs and windows of London are rippling with red-white-and-blue; even the poorest dwelling shows its three-hap'ny flag. Every street-organ is playing and every boy whistling, Leslie Stuart's *Soldiers of the Queen*. Schoolboys are wearing in the lapels of their coats enamel portrait-buttons of the Queen and the Royal Family. One is taken round the main streets at dusk to see the "illuminations"--just fairy-lamps of candle, oil or gas, but lighting the London of that time with the superlative of carnival blaze. London is celebrating the Record Reign and sixty years of what it thought was Progress, never guessing that more progress was to be packed into the next thirty years than the whole previous hundred years could show.

That is the London I saw and felt when I first became consciously aware of London. I had been running about it for some years before that, but it is from the Diamond Jubilee that I date remembered detail. It was a London that still held many of the fixtures and much of the atmosphere of what has come to be known as the Dickens' London. A London of horse-trams with halfpenny fares, and of hansom cabs; of crystalline bells and spattering hoofs. A London with winters of slush and fog of a richer sort than any known to-day, and summers of dust and clam; the slush and dust being its heritage from the horse-traffic. A London of silk hats, frock-coats, beards, curled moustaches, "choker" collars, leg-of-mutton sleeves, veils, bonnets, and, threading through these gigmanities, as herald of revolt, an execrated vixen in bloomers riding a bicycle. A London of solid homes, which regarded the introduction of flat-life as something Not Quite Nice; in fact, Fast. A London in which the head of the house still carved the joint at his Sunday table in the presence of his six or seven sons and daughters. A London of low buildings against which Queen Anne's Mansions was a sky-scraper. A London of lost corners; of queer nooks and rookeries; of curling lanes and derelict squares, unknown to the rest of London, and often, it seemed, forgotten by their local Councils. A London which, away from the larger streets, held pools of utter darkness, and terraces of crumbling caverns, and infinitudes of mist which called one as surely as the ranges to penetrate their fastness. A London whose roads were mainly granite setts, and therefore a London of turmoil and clatter. A London in which the more prosperous business men drove to their offices in their broughams. A London in which the first cars were appearing, to the puzzled scorn of the majority of the brougham-owners. "Never make a Do of those things. People never give up horses for *those*." A London in which particular trades and callings still wore particular clothes, and which still nourished public "characters" and eccentrics. A London in which strong language, of a strength that would blanch these outspoken times, was used by certain men of all social classes. A London where entertaining in restaurants was just beginning to displace the more pleasant but (for the hostess) more troublesome custom of entertaining at one's own table. A London in which paper money, save in the five-ten-twenty series, was unthought of. A London in which a golden sovereign would give you a quiet evening's entertainment of a kind which five pound-notes could not buy to-day. A London which, as befitted a great metropolis, had nine evening papers against to-day's meagre three. A London which was the centre of an Empire, and knew it. And a London which, in a few of its nerves, was beginning to be aware of the end of an epoch and of the New this and the New that.

    Districts then were emphatically themselves; little islands washed by various alien waters which never penetrated inland. East was East and West was West. The foreign quarters *were* foreign. Soho was beginning to be anybody's country, but ordinary Londoners were seldom seen in the Italian streets of Back Hill, Eyre Street Hill or Warner Street; or in the recesses of the Ghetto, or in Limehouse or the Dutch streets of Spitalfields. Few of them knew the inner courts of Notting Dale and Hoxton, and artists and poets were never seen in the taverns of Bankside or Shadwell. All these places were then enclosed communities. So were many of the central districts. Chelsea was Chelsea and Streatham was Streatham. Cromwell Road knew nothing of Barnsbury, nor Stratford of Dulwich Village; and only a few cyclists had ever discovered the end of Finchley Road. Regent Street was then an "expensive" street, and even Oxford Street had not yet become the rendezvous of suburban housewives. Each district had its own perceptible key and maintained it. If a man lived in a mews he was a working-man, and if he lived in Mount Street he was a man of quality. If he lived in Bloomsbury he was hard-up, and if he lived in Prince's Gate he was wealthy. Kensington was notably Kensington and had little to do with the other side of the Park, the not-quite Bayswater; and a young man of Jermyn Street would not know of the existence of a place called Islington. The West End was still the West End. Change was being felt, and, in a small way, its seclusion was, by its own invitation, being invaded by people who could be "used." But commercial establishments had not disrupted the stateliness of its squares and streets. A suggestion that trams should run along the Embankment and buses along Park Lane; that one might open a theatre in Whitehall, cheap tea-shops in Bond Street, offices in Carlton House Terrace, entertainments of "animated photographs" in Curzon Street, and the world's chief wireless station in Portland Place, would have been too facetious to evoke even a smile.

It is a habit with the middle-aged--almost a symptom of middle-age--to hold that things in their youth were superior to things of the present; and it is true that in just a few matters the London of the early years of this century did have some points on the London of to-day. But only a few. Physically, it was dingy, and the general scene was by no means so fluent and coloured as it is to-day. It had far fewer pleasures and public amenities; most of the "gaiety" that one hears about took place within doors, and the public places caught only its aftermath in the form of reeling and uproarious young men. It was a city of extreme wealth, solid comfort, and extreme poverty; and these three estates agreed that things always had been like that and always would be. Often the third lived within a stone's-throw of the first, but in mutual indifference, never crossing each other's boundary. The Social Conscience, spurred by the Fabian Society, was then only beginning its first efforts at closing the cleft between them.

But the spirit of the people was more at ease. They had not then been crushed by blows at Imperial prestige and by forebodings of economic collapse, and if they had fewer pleasures they had fewer worries. You would not have guessed it by their faces. They were a stolid-looking, self-centred lot, and made no display of their content. They did not go about crying "Let's be gay. Let's make whoopee." Life was sufficiently agreeable without manufactured festivity. They were wedged in security, and had no need for war-cries or for songs urging them to keep their hearts up. Those "cheery" songs we are hearing to-day are a symptom of our condition. When a man asks in a loud voice: "Who's afraid of the big bad wolf?" there is but one answer to the question. The fact that the question is asked supplies the answer, which is: "*You* are." In those days there was no big bad wolf on the horizon, and the wild party was not thought of, either as amusement or as despairing resource. There was no demand for a brighter London. They thought, the poor dears of those days, that their dingy London with its isolated cylinders of social life was already bright. George Edwardes was giving them the new light entertainment of "musical comedy"; the opera was an apparently immutable fixture of the London year; the Empire and Alhambra supplied them with traditional ballet-spectacle; the "halls" were in full flower; the park bands were playing Sousa's Marches; and Leicester Square and Piccadilly Circus were key-notes of "frivolity"--a word of the period.

As for night-life, that was an indulgence for well-to-do young men and their seniors, and a few "daring" girls. There were decent nightclubs for those of ample means, and others of a wholly disreputable sort. There were none for the middle-classes, and if they had been started it is doubtful whether the middle-classes of that period would have patronised them. They might have felt them unnecessary, since licensing regulations were not what they are to-day. Most restaurants served after-theatre suppers, and were open till one in the morning, and in the days before taxis and cars that was late enough for the somewhat heavy folk who had offices to attend.

For the rest, the amusements of these folk of about the end of the century would seem to the present young of a simple order. They stood between the *Yellow Book* period and the postwar period. Their appetites were normal, and they did not cry "for madder music and for stronger wine." When they went out to dinner they did not ask the restaurateur to add to his duties those of music-hall manager, M.C., and clown. They asked him to supply an agreeable, well-served meal, and sound wines. Any other pleasures they supplied themselves. In those days people still talked. They used, not interjections and repetitions of Society's latest epithet, but conversation; and in most restaurants they could talk in a level voice and be heard. A few of the bars around Leicester Square--Provence, Café de l'Europe, Gambrinus, etc.--had orchestras, but they were not found in many restaurants. Even at the pioneer middle-class night-club, which arrived a few years before the War, when Austin Harrison and Mdme. Strindberg opened the Cave of the Golden Calf, even there, talk was mainly the thing. The term night-club had to wait a decade or more before it became synonymous with overcrowding and lack-lustre racket. Elderly people were complaining of the pace of London life, as elderly people have always been doing from the time of John Lydgate. Actually it was as it always is when regarded in relation to its period--just a little slower than it should have been.

The great spread in recent years of public pleasure and outdoor entertainment is an overdue development; but, coming so suddenly, it has had the effect of leaving people, when they cannot get this public pleasure, in mid-air and at a loss. They do not know how to amuse themselves. The modern provision of mass-amusement, and the mechanical inventions which bring it almost to their doors, have distracted them from the effort of providing their own. Six people making merry in a drawing-room or parlour, if they know how to do it, will always be individually merrier than any one of six hundred people sharing a common merriment in a restaurant or hall. But indoor, self-made amusement is now regarded as "too much bother."

In the past, people were more independent, ready to be themselves instead of seeking to be a matrix of everybody else. Sober as they were in their dress and their setting, their blood, I think, was richer and their nerves stouter. They were more ebullient than their children of to-day. Bread and circuses have made us tame; amenable to all sorts of direct and indirect propaganda. Our London is much younger and brisker in spirit than theirs, and wears a brighter countenance. But in relation to theirs it is as cocktails and sherry to Margaux and Chambertin.

Even when I began to be an active atom of London life--in the early nineteen-noughts--this Margaux and Chambertin tone prevailed, and I came to manhood in a London of stolid security and sanguine outlook. A century, in its social and spiritual significance, seldom begins at its calendar point; and the early years of the twentieth century were infused by a strong hang-over from the nineteenth. Just as the nineteenth century did not begin until 1840, and spent its childhood with the last vapours of the eighteenth, so the twentieth century took some time to adjust itself; though it took only half the time taken by the nineteenth. The early years were an interregnum between the rule of the old and the new. The death of Victoria brought a sudden release of bottled-up ideas and activities. Much of it led nowhere;

it was a sort of out-of-school burst; a manifestation of *"now* we can do things." And through the Edward decade people did things. But those things were mainly a trying-out; we were not really in the twentieth century. Too many fashions, tastes and prejudices of the nineteenth remained with us to prevent our really going ahead into a new century and a new life. There was a fresher and freer tone in London life, but it did not carry any reconstruction or redistribution of values. It was merely an easing and brightening of the old. The austere schoolmistress was gone and had been replaced by a genial, easy-going master; but the school was much the same. Victoria's death was not the end of the nineteenth century, nor was Edward's. The true end of that century, and the beginning of the twentieth and of new-age growing-pains, was the end of the Great War. Not until 1920 did London enter upon its new era of structural and spiritual change.

Thus, in writing of London before the war one has a feeling of writing of the London of last century. And really one is. In talking to young people about London and London life before the war, and the things we did in that London, I find that they cannot regard them as part of twentieth-century life. *They* are twentieth century, and the London they know is the only twentieth-century London. We middle-aged folk, who started our boyhood ramblings about the London of 1904-5, they regard as stragglers from the Victorian age; which we are. Still, we had the privilege of witnessing the changeover, and it is something to have seen. As I began looking at London in

1897, and, save for holidays, have been constantly in attendance upon it, I have had London under observation through nearly four decades. Those years have been years of such radical and violent change in London life and the ways of the Londoner that no similar span of its long life can have known such a transformation. The differences between the London of the year of Diamond Jubilee and the London of 1934 are, I think, even more marked than the differences between the London of James II and the London of the Regency. Certainly they are of wider variety and scope than the memory of any Victorian centenarian could embrace.

The processes by which these differences have arrived have been so stealthy and so minute that to the constant Londoner, like myself, who has lived through them, they are often untraceable. A few of the larger junctions which register departure-points for change stand out, and among these I would set:

> The Underground Railway.
> The electric tram and motor-bus.
> The making of Aldwych and Kingsway.
> The spread of service flats.
> The coming of popular cafés and popular hotels.
> The opening of Selfridge's.
> The new social amenities of streets and parks.
> The use of tarmac and re-inforced concrete.
> The brightening of Sunday.

But the sources of the change in social behaviour and outlook remain as obscure as the sources of the seasonal change in women's dress. Mode arrives among us, nobody knows whence. We find ourselves doing the same things and saying the same things, and no person or group of persons is responsible for this. It is an immigration from the invisible. Social history is a record of these immigrations, and not even the philosophers can decide for us the wherefore.

In the past forty years we of middle-age have witnessed many of these abrupt swerves from mode to mode, and because they are general and affect us all we do not notice their clean break from the recent mode. From the same cause we do not notice the abrupt changes in the London scene, and it is only when we look back that we realise how many changes have happened under our eyes. We have seen Society in its well-conducted, almost demure period; in its inane Bright-Young-Thing period; and within the last year or so we have seen it swerve again from the Mrs. Merrick note to the sensible and responsible. We have seen music-halls go, and movies arrive and develop to talkies. We have seen women's fashions pass from the bonnet and trailing skirt, through the hobble skirt and Merry Widow hat, the shirt-blouse, and bee-hive hat, the knee-length skirt of the twenties, the Eton crop and the shingle, to the bare legs and beret of the thirties. We have seen girls in the parks, at one time shrouded from neck to ankle, and at another in little but bathing-slips. We have seen the last days of Rosherville and the first days of the Lido. We have watched the blurred pageantry of the Votes for Women processions, and have seen women reach Parliament and all other departments of the nation's councils. We have seen London Pride, which went into decay for the greater part of the nineteenth century, reassert itself. We have seen streets of smoky brick become streets of glistening concrete. We have seen the outward thrust of business from the centre of town do as much in a few years towards slum-clearance as had been done in the previous fifty. We have seen commerce dress itself with dignity, and endow London with the Kubla Khan domes and towers of the P.L.A. building, the Shell-Mex building, the I.C.I. building, Transport House, and the new hotels of Park Lane. We have seen rural villages become suburbs. We have seen spots that, in our childhood, were "in the country," become part of the route of central London buses. We have seen our London, which had its limits at Barking, Shepherd's Bush, Croydon and Finchley, grow to a London which is London until you are beyond Romford, Uxbridge, Epsom or Watford.

Every Londoner, I think, will agree with me that it is as hard to say when or how the change happened as to say when a plant increased from six inches to seven inches. And will agree with me that the chief material agents, acting under our very noses, were undoubtedly petrol and electricity. The electric tram, the motor-bus, the extension of the Tube railways, the cheap private car--these widened man's radius and gave an acceleration to his natural desire for movement. From this power of swift and frequent change sprang all the developments in physical London and its tempo, and in the Londoner's home habits, outdoor habits, and amusements.

Some of these developments, as I say, the born Londoner hardly perceives. He accepts them as having always been, and is not aware, until he definitely considers them, that they are key-points of a new order. For a true appraisal of these developments one must look elsewhere. One must use the eye of a returned Londoner who went into the wilderness at the end of last century, and has had no news of London or of any other great city. First, one might puzzle him with a little examination-paper on London features. Something like this:

> What is a Corner House?
> Where is the Ritz?
> What is Wardour Street noted for?
> Define a subway, an escalator, a news-theatre, a Labour Exchange.
> Where is the North Circular Road?
> What is Croydon chiefly known for?
> Where is the Garden Suburb?
> What is the quickest way from Charing Cross to Edgware?
> What is a flatlet?
> From what point does the night coach leave London for Newcastle?
> Where is the London Lido?

When he had given up most of these, as he would, one could set him wandering. What would first strike him? No doubt he would turn, as most homing exiles do, to Piccadilly Circus, and if he reached it at night he could be excused for thinking he had taken the wrong turning. But before he could reach it he would have taken a random eye-cast at the general face of London. If he arrived at Waterloo, and looked upon London from the other side, he would see a very different scape from that which he last saw. Some of the old points would reassure him--Big Ben and Victoria Tower; Cleopatra's Needle; Somerset House--but he would be as astonished by the staring brilliance of the new buildings of the Embankment as one of us would be if he were transported to Mr. Wells' City of the Future. Yet with all the difference he would know it for a *London* scape. It has set itself between river and sky with the air of having always belonged there. It is still London, but London rejuvenated. A more vigorous London; no longer solid and complacent, but challenging and thrusting. A London of firmer line and harder feature. A London no longer keeping its brightness to private display, but bringing whatever it has to the streets. A London that lives no longer in splendid mansions, but in flats; that follows personally the simple life and showers magnificence into the common stock. Formerly London's beautiful buildings were private homes, and for public buildings anything was held to be good enough. This custom is now reversed, and public and commercial affairs are transacted in halls of marble whose faces shine with civic dignity.

In a casual glance at this new London, one petty detail would perhaps give evidence of the passing of years more strongly than any major factor. There is one section of the London scene which affects us more than we know, though we see it only as we see the paving we walk on. As many people subconsciously remember a first tour of France, not by any star of the guidebook's constellation; not by some great château or bridge or cathedral, but by the face of that baby who, this quarter-century, has been haunting the French sky-line for the benefit of the soap of M. Cadum; so one of the mnemonic notes that call up London to the Londoner is its public advertisements. My first childish impression of London was not of a city of people, but of a city of lamps and the lit windows of shops. My second was of a city of advertisements. I am told that it was a habit of mine, as soon as I had learned to read, to spell out all the advertisements when riding in trains and buses and trams. So, when I recall the London of my childhood, almost the first entrants in the troupe of memories are--Nixey's Black Lead; Reckitt's Blue; Hinde's Curlers; Sapolio; Epps' Cocoa; Brooke's Soap Monkey Brand; Frame Food; and Whelpton's Purifying Pills.

Many of the commodities whose names, forty years ago, were truly household words, are still announcing themselves by the newest trans-Atlantic methods, but our homing exile would miss a number which were to him a fixed feature of the London scene, and would miss everywhere the restrained, almost bashful note of their advertising. The pictorial side of that advertising was commonly painful; the influence of James Pryde and William Nicholson and Steinlen was limited in its range, and it was long before commerce generally had followed the lead given by those who employed these artists. The letter-press was usually a blunt claim of superiority--"Drink Somebody's Cocoa. It Is The Best." Or "Somebody's Soap. Good For The Complexion." In its place he would find a deft thrust at his weaknesses. In the new stones and forms of London he would be able to perceive the solid city of his youth, but on its face--that part of it rented for advertising--which he had left demure, he would find grins, grimaces, pouts, leers and winks. Only the presence of Eros, the London Pavilion and the Criterion, would reassure him that he really had found Piccadilly Circus. In his day it was known as "the centre of the world." To-day it is known to a too-large and too-clamant section as the Premier Publicity Site. Such advertising as it carried in his day was no more than a gentle gesture of the hand indicating the excellence of this or that over other kinds of this or that. The whole Circus now is a series of ear-racking screams and eye-smiting gyrations against which the extreme contortions of the Jack Puddings of Bartholomew Fair would be almost modest. Yet it still manages to remain Piccadilly Circus, and for this generation of London boys it will be what it was for their fathers and grandfathers. The Strand, too, he would hardly know, for changes here have been more violent than in any other one street. Forty or fifty of the features which made the Strand of his youth are gone. Lowther Arcade and Exeter Hall, prominent features of his time, were in their last gasp when I began work in 1902; I just remember seeing them. Aldwych and Kingsway were in the pangs of birth as a heap of ruins, and the new Gaiety Theatre and Gaiety Hotel were only being thought of. Notable points that he would miss are Morley's Hotel, which was round the corner in Trafalgar Square; the Golden Cross; Haxell's little hotel in Exeter Street; Terry's Theatre; the old Strand Theatre; Wych Street; the old Tivoli; the Hotel Cecil; and perhaps Burgess' Fish Sauce Shop, the old tongue-twister. The Gaiety Hotel came and went before we had time to get used to it.

When I first knew the Strand the project of widening it was not even talked of. With that widening the whole structure of the street has changed within the recollection of those who are still in their teens. As I say, it has throughout its life been marked for constant change. As the High Street, reflecting always the contemporary taste of everyday London, it is never settled for long. The Strand of the nineties is now almost obliterated, and the Strand of even a later period has suffered so much pulling about that for the middle-aged it is a new street. Very little of that Strand of 1909, which the music-halls of that year were inviting us to go down, remains to-day, and the little that does appears in a new dress.

Yet, like Piccadilly Circus, it retains enough of that genius of personality which, in the past, carried its name in many songs round the English-speaking world. It is not now "the place for fun and noise; all among the girls and boys." It is hardly the pleasure-street it once was. That title, if by pleasure we mean theatres and restaurants, should belong to-day to Shaftesbury Avenue, which holds more theatres than any other street and borders that congerie of restaurants, Soho. But Shaftesbury Avenue has never fully been on the London map. It has all the qualifications, but somehow it lacks that corporate, close-facetted personality which, through all changes, distinguishes other streets and fixes them in public association. Just as one man with marked ability and an excellent direction of it yet fails to succeed, while his fellow, with a mere dab of ability, becomes a public figure, so Shaftesbury Avenue has missed that fame which has been granted rightly to the Strand and somewhat strangely to the void and spiritless Trafalgar Square. Maybe this fame, like the fame of so many London features, rests on tradition only; maybe the public honours certain streets, not for what they are, but for what they were fifty, a hundred, or two hundred years ago. Cheapside is much more spoken of than Queen Victoria Street; Pall Mall than St. James' Street; and Bond Street than Jermyn Street. Maybe, too, the name is a factor. "Shaftesbury Avenue" hardly lends itself to song as The Strand, Piccadilly and Leicester Square do. The Strand may change as often and as sharply as it pleases; it will still be London's High Street, an allusion-point in all London talk and a cog in the wheels of all London memories. In just one point it remains as it was when our exile last saw it. It is still a man's street. Almost anything a man wants can be got here. It never was a woman's street and to-day, as formerly, it has almost nothing for her. But as she has Oxford Street, Regent Street, St. Paul's Churchyard, and Kensington High Street almost wholly to herself she can hardly object to the segregation of this one street to the male.

Wherever our homing exile might go he would find, save in the isolated corners, radical change. He would find the City region not so compact as in his day; he would find it reaching to the east and north-east. He would find Leadenhall Street a street of white palaces, and would no doubt be as shocked at finding that the Bank of England has gone *sur-realiste* as if he had found the Sphinx going coy. He would find Fleet Street almost wholly rebuilt. In Soho he would find that the quiet curio shops he knew have been replaced by the flaunting windows of film companies. He would find the bookstalls loaded with papers he had not heard of, and would ask in vain for many old favourites. He would miss the most thrilling spectacle of his London--the splendid charge of the old greys which drew our fire-engines; but might find compensation in the dashing cars of the Flying Squad. He would miss the pastry-cook's, and would find in its place not merely tea-shops, which were beginning in his day, but Byzantine palaces where people may enjoy for sixpence such surroundings as were formerly reserved for the wealthy.

An early impression would be the absence of abject and paraded poverty. If he went to the Embankment and a few other places at midnight, he would soon learn that London has as much poverty as in his day; but he would remember that in his day one saw barefooted children in utter rags, and workless men, with knees showing through their torn trousers, eating refuse from dustbins. He would not see men in such expressive destitution now; there is food to-day for all who will ask for it; but poverty remains, hidden away in back rooms in back streets. Nor would he see any of the former display of wealth. London is still one of the richest cities of the world, if not the richest, but the rich and privileged, within the last twenty years, have learned something of good taste and have renounced ostentation. Everybody to-day, whatever his rank, tries to be a "reg'lar fellow."

He would miss Earl's Court, but in its place he would find mixed bathing in the Serpentine, an open-air theatre in Regent's Park, greyhound tracks, speedway tracks, hundreds of cinemas in every style of magnificence from Assyrian to Renaissance, a palace of dance in every suburb; and, in short, twenty times more public pleasure than his day had dreamed of. He would appreciate the increase of colour in the streets--not only in the people's clothes, but in shop-windows, house-fronts and doorways. He would remember the Squares he had left with their enclosures of dreary evergreens (or evergreys) and he would see Squares of green lawns and gay flower-beds. If he had come from Southern Europe he would find the London Sunday still a somewhat heavy affair, but he would not find it quite so Calvinistic as the Sunday of his youth. He would note a happier tone about the people in the parks, and a holiday spirit in the parties of youth setting out for country rambles.

If he talked to this youth at all he would note the absence of one symbol of the London of his time--the old Cockney slang. He would listen in vain for the crudely picturesque phrases which once were the language of the streets. In place of them he would hear a less picturesque but more piquant slang borrowed from American movies and American vaudeville turns. The Cockney's Yuss or Yerce is now Yeah. Things that used to be A Bit of All Right are now O.K. Where he used to ask if you Saw What He Meant, he now asks if you Get Him? Where he used to urge you to Buck Up, he now urges you to Snap Into It. Back-slang has gone, rhyming-slang has gone, and the "ag" language has gone. Brooklynese is the new Volapuk. With this change has come a change in the common London voice. Broadcasting and the talkies may have helped towards this change. The whining voice which was generally heard in our exile's day is now seldom heard. The tone may not be elegant, but it is crisper; more emphatic. The London face, too, would appear a little strange to him against his memories. Each social period has its special voice and face, and the face of the middle-aged Londoner today is markedly different from that of his fellow of thirty or forty years ago. One saw then beards and moustaches on plump faces, and easy, unquestioning eyes. To-day the face is thinner, the features more eager, the eyes keener. Partly this is due to the general spread of exercise and the outdoor week-end, partly to the accelerated pace of London life, and partly to economic anxiety.

Belgravia and South Kensington, which in his day were of high importance, he would find much changed both in appearance and significance; while he would find little in Bloomsbury to recall the drab and downcast district he had left. He would find that it has punned upon its name and preened its face and filled itself with blossom. The see-saw of London values has been working vigorously in the past few decades, and the obscure has become brilliant and the brilliant obscure. Many of the restaurants famous in his day are gone or are no longer in fashion. Those in fashion he would find of a new type. The qualities demanded by fashion thirty years ago are not now demanded. Cabaret, then almost unknown inEngland, is more important than cuisine, and the gourmet is a disappearing type. He needs leisure for his growth, and to-day people are not inclined to linger and savour their pleasures. They taste only. Dining must be worked in with other things--with dancing and a show; and sitting over the port when you might be dancing is regarded as a waste of that time which nobody seems to have. He would find that the leisured classes have lost the art of leisure. They must always be Doing Something. Wherever they may be they are always Going On somewhere else. Even in club-land he would find only a semblance of the old repose. He would perceive a brisker rhythm, a wider outlook. In the social clubs he would be shocked to find a profane intrusion of business talk.

Meals, in both restaurants and the average home, he would find shorter and better selected. Ceremony, save in a few circles, has been banished. Even etiquette has no exact definitions to-day, and Good Form has become a topic for the facetious columnists. Barley water is not only more favoured than the heavier wines of the early years, but is increasingly displacing, especially in summer, the cocktail or sherry of to-day. At lunch and supper the snack has supplanted the three- or four-course meal, and many of the young seem to live wholly on nibbles of *hors d'œuvres*.

These changes, in some degree, are welcome. They have made the whole tone of London life lighter and easier. The new century demanded an adjustment of social customs, and a physical tenuity, and the Londoner supplied them. To meet the new celerity those who were stout went to great daily pains to get thin. The slimming craze is not a beauty craze; its purpose is more rapid movement. The development of the car enabled us to travel at speed, and we have made speed the measure for all the little occasions of our day. We even talk more rapidly. And our talk is no longer confined to commonplaces and a few rigid topics. We now discuss Everything. There seems to be no taboo, not even in public places. There was already, in our exile's day, under the influence of the *fin-de-siècle* novelists, a tendency, among the daring, to a more liberal and honest outlook, but he would, I fancy, be surprised by the freedom of conversation among the very young, and the casual allusions to "certain" matters. The Victorians knew all about those matters, but saw no reason for making a song about them. To-day we are so anxious to make songs about them that we often make the song before we really know.

Some of the features that are gone our exile would regard as good riddances, but one almost-vanished feature he would, if he were any sort of fellow, regret. When he left London it had, around its centre, fourteen music-halls, and in the near suburbs thirty more. To-day, though variety entertainment is still to be had, and of a more slick and polished quality than formerly, it is not the natural living growth it was in the past. One feels that it is making a deliberate stand for recognition against cabaret and radio and the talkies, and that, though it is finding a public, the curve of favour is towards the others. Attempts have been made to revive it, but it belonged to an age, and though you may revive the features of an age you cannot revive its spirit. The young, of course, do not miss the music-hall; their particular phase of light entertainment is cabaret, and fifty years hence they will be talking wistfully of the good days of the nineteen-thirties when cabaret was spontaneous and rich. Meantime, they listen wearily to their elders talking of music-hall, and cannot understand why the old things should be so sentimental about that rough, raucous form of entertainment, or why they should prefer the simple songs of those dead halls--part of the native poetry of London--to the cute torch- songs and jazz-crooning imported from the States.

The first quarter of this century, indeed, may be known to history as London's American Phase, since the major part of the many and rapid changes it has suffered may be traced to America. Our tube railways we owe to America. The bulk of our entertainment is American in quality and largely in personnel. All our latest hotels derive from American models. Our snack-bars and all-night supper-stands are pirated from America. Our electric night-signs are an American idea. Our street songs are American. Our popular press models itself upon American journalism, and on our bookstalls English periodicals lie smothered and half-seen under piles of American magazines. Our newest buildings, where they are not German or Swedish, are American. Our one-way streets and automatic traffic controls are American. Where we knew little individual shops we now find giant Stores, run on the American plan; and the threepenny and sixpenny store is so much a feature of almost every large street, both in and out of London, that we almost forget its American origin. The new verve of our social occasions, and the mixing of all classes, are American traits. Even the country has not escaped, and on the main roads outside London, where we used to find English inns, we now find gaudy shacks working under the American title of "road-houses."

These importations, as I say, are not without value; they are responsible for that lighter and easier tone. London needed a certain quickening. It was getting set, and though the war shook it up a little, and shuffled its values, the tendency, after the war, was to relapse to the *status quo ante.* The American yeast, working constantly upon it these last twenty years, has done so much good that we now regard the zest and pungency of London life, which the States gave us, as our own growth. It has had many of these exotic phases, but it takes them only as a tonic for its self-expression. In the late seventeenth century it was pervaded by French styles. In the middle eighteenth everything Italian was correct. In the middle nineteenth it went all German. What it will be after its American Phase is hardly guessable: there seems very little choice in the way of new civilisations.

One group of features of the London scene our exile would find almost as he left them. While the rest of London takes doses of Fifth Avenue or Michigan Boulevard or Wilhelmstrasse, the nineteenth century remains with us in our dear, dim, smelly railway stations. Waterloo and Victoria have done a little towards bringing themselves into the modern scheme and edging towards Grand Central Terminal; and Marylebone always had light and space. But the others. . . . Think of London Bridge, on which John Davidson wrote a poem in praise of the perfect example "of what a railway station shouldn't be." Think of the external face of King's Cross--or try not to. Think of Fenchurch Street and Liverpool Street, and see whether, from them, you can catch some glimmering of the inwardness of the Londoner. Think of the architectural grace of Charing Cross. When they will be reconstructed and made as agreeable to the eye, and as convenient for the stranger, as our Tube stations, I don't know. Since they have lasted so many years in their Victorian dress, I doubt if even my infant godson will live long enough to see an elegant King's Cross. Indeed, if they last much longer as they are I would resent any attempt to bring them into these times: I would prefer to see the Society for the Preservation of Ancient Monuments take them over.

Looking around this cleaner, lighter, half-American London, our exile would no doubt be surprised by its new profiles. Not only in the Strand but in many another highway design has been at work. When as a boy I was trotting about London there were no uniform streets. The vista of even the great highways was broken and incongruous. There were no such lines as are offered to-day by Kingsway, Regent Street, the western half of Oxford Street, and the new Leadenhall Street. Demolition and rebuilding were then matters of private whim, and planning was only beginning to be considered. The Strand particularly was a jumble of low buildings and tall buildings, old shops and new shops; some bright, some dingy--the new shops often the dingier; some dignified and comely, some mere utilitarian erections; some jutting forward, some lying back. There were bits of the late eighteenth century, bits of the early nineteenth, much of the middle nineteenth, with the late nineteenth muscling in, and here and there some timid thrust of the "new" style which thought it was going to be twentieth century, until the real twentieth century knocked it out. We did not apologise to our visitors for this jumble; we exhibited it as typical London. We felt, as each generation has felt, that it was the real London at last, the complete expression of the city. But to-day we ride in taxis and buses through

American streets and German streets and Scandinavian streets, and proudly show them to our visitors and say--"This is London." For so strong is its power of absorbing alien importations into its essence and making them peculiar to itself, that to-day, when on all sides we see New York avenues and Stockholm buildings, we can still claim that their space and light are the expression of ourselves. London has woven them into its mighty fabric, and for the young of to-day they will live as permanent symbols of London.

This power of absorption may best be realised by taking a distant view of the city. Go to some high point--Highgate Archway, Shooter's Hill, the top of St. Paul's, or the front of the Crystal Palace. From any of these points the silhouette to be seen is generally, though on a larger scale, the silhouette which was always seen. The changes in figure and feature which seem so comprehensive when one is in the streets are, from these heights, hardly perceptible. With all the new country ground taken in by its rapid growth, with all the destruction and reconstruction, it has the figure and the personality with which it began. It has grown as man grows, true to its early form and style; and in 1934 its shape is still that of the rough diamond shown on Norden's map of the late sixteenth century. After all the frenzy of change which has marked the last forty years, only here and there does some new tower or glittering commercial Pantheon corrupt the old silhouette; and then only trivially. There, point by point, are all the features which, in the last hundred years, have come to signify London throughout the world--Big Ben, the Victoria Tower, St. Paul's, the Monument, and around the last the spires of many churches which our greatest of grandfathers saw. There it lies, a huge and sprawling growth, but still in an unbroken line, from newt, as it were, to crocodile. As of all great beings, one may say that the more it changes the more it remains itself.

PEOPLE

There was a time within recent memory when the London streets were, or seemed to be, full of "characters." Some of these were celebrated by the press and became known outside London. There was "Spring Onions," the Stepney poet. There was Craig, the cricket poet of the Oval. There was Humphreys, the Paternoster Row bookseller, of picturesque appearance, who decorated his shop with blue-pencilled exhortations from the Scriptures. There was the man who haunted the Strand and announced by a card in his hat that he was from Australia, seeking his lost daughter. There was the man who sold the *Pall Mall Gazette* at the bottom of Regent Street, dressed in the clothes given him by club-men--silk hat, frock coat, watered silk waistcoat, etc. And scores of others.

But of late years, under the general movement for uniforms and uniformity, they have been slowly passing from the London scene, and the only examples to be seen to-day are those who address the crowds from the rostrums of Hyde Park on Sunday afternoons. The war, which altered or obliterated so many factors and features of London life, obliterated the "characters." Old dodderers like myself miss them. They were a condiment to the every-dayness of the streets. They lived as they wished to live; behaved as they wished to behave; dressed as they wished to dress. Standardisation had not then set it, and the first ten years of this century marked perhaps the last phase of individualism. In those days variety was permitted and encouraged. To-day we must be homogeneous or perish.

Character was displayed not only by these quaint, obscure eccentrics of the streets. It was also displayed by the serious and famous. The outstanding figures in the various walks of life were not too shy to proclaim, by style and habit, their difference. Politicians, musicians, actors, lawyers, poets, bookmakers, comedians--each type announced its detachment from the common run, and lent the crowd a touch that made it a carnival crowd rather than a marching army. They recognised as keenly as anybody of to-day that all men are brothers. They saw no reason for trying to pass themselves off as a twin. Distinguished people then *looked* distinguished. To-day, at any gathering of the intellectually distinguished, half the company look like bankers and the other half like shop-assistants. One or two survivors of the old guard are with us, and in a world of sameness remain defiantly picturesque. One glance at Mr. Arthur Machen tells us that here is the romantic story-teller, and one glance at Mr. Augustus John discloses the painter. Thirty years ago most writers, painters, and musicians blazed themselves against the herd, and the Café Royal in those days was an assembly of strikingly personal costume, hair-dressing and deportment. Many of the figures, it must be admitted, looked far more distinguished than they really were, and it was perhaps this intrusion of the amateur, self-made Bohemian which led the artists and writers to react towards bourgeois formality.

The actor and comedian, too, presented themselves to the world in a sort of challenge costume, and made no attempt to be mistaken for young men about town. The actor's appearance announced the theatre, and the comedian's the music-hall--then two separate worlds which did not meet. The rank-and-file actors haunted the Strand, Bedford Street and Garrick Street. The music-hall people gathered around Waterloo Station and York Road, and on Sunday mornings at Brixton. Newspaper men also were recognisable from other folk, and from other kinds of literary men. The popular novelist was only beginning to break into Fleet Street with "special articles," and at that time one would not have mistaken him for a pressman, or vice versa. Fleet Street, throughout its history as newspaper-street, had its constant pageant of picturesque figures, but I think we saw the last of them in the nineteen-twenties. In this last group were Arthur Machen, T. W. H. Crosland, Randal Charlton and Hannen Swaffer. All of them were, and two still are, men of an "appearance" and *panacherie* too rare in these days when potential personalities masquerade as so many peas in a pod. Those who are old enough to compare the diversified group that used to gather in the defunct "Green Dragon" with the group that gathered until lately in Poet's Corner of Poppin's Court, will realise that what we have gained in conformity we have lost in piquancy. No man, whatever his talents, has the power to be both correct *and* interesting, and when the memoirs of the twenties and thirties come to be written they will make rather thin reading. They may be helped by the follies and stupidities of the immediate post-war period, but so far as personal "character" is concerned, the diarists will have as hard a job to give zest to their records as current cartoonists have to make pungent pictures out of commonplace figures and faces. (Though it is possible they may find a relish to their narratives in Sir Thomas Beecham.)

In those early years the mixing of classes and professions was only beginning. Clubs, taverns and restaurants still preserved a special and regular clientèle, and strollers from outside were strollers from outside. Bohemia was as watertight an enclosure as the inner circles of Society. You were in it or not, and neither Society nor Bohemia displayed any desire to enter the other's preserves. To-day, there are few preserves, and the social Bohemia and the arty Bohemia are constantly mingling. Few restaurants keep any special note; they are just restaurants, cheap or expensive. One could once be sure that of the company in a certain restaurant every man was connected with either the theatre or sport. In another restaurant, that every man was somewhere concerned with the literary world. In another, that every man was engaged in some capacity in the law. To-day everybody goes everywhere, and in any restaurant you may get if not the best at least a sample of all worlds. The arty Bohemia was then fixed in Chelsea, with a rather more wealthy and more formal offshoot at St. John's

Wood. The Fitzroy and Charlotte Street Bohemia did not arise until after the war. Bohemia is an unsatisfactory word, since it conveys to most people something deliberate and cultivated, connected with drink and loose morals, whereas truly it is a state of mind rather than a way of living. But there is no other word immediately available to cover a mode which disregards herd-thought, herd-behaviour and herd-attitudes. Fleet Street had its own Bohemia, but by the time I knew The Street it was conventional and business-like. I am too young to have known the Rhymers' Club at the "Cheshire Cheese" where gathered Dowson, Lionel Johnson and other men of the nineties; too young to have known even the later group--The Songsters--and too young to have known that rather knockabout but very capable group which made the *Sporting Times:* John Corlett, Arthur Binstead, Edward Mott, Newnham-Davis, Arnold Goldberg, and others whose names escape me.

The literary world, at the time I began my wanderings, was beginning to move from Paternoster Row to Covent Garden, and very soon Covent Garden was a centre for publishers, literary agents and magazines. From 1907 to 1930 Henrietta Street was almost wholly literary, and to a young beginner in literature it was full of interest. Around mid-day, in the years before the war, one might see W. L. Courtney and Arthur Waugh coming from the offices of Chapman & Hall; H. W. Massingham dashing into the offices of *The Nation;* Edward Garnett carrying a bag of MSS. to the offices of Duckworth; Sir Home Gordon, cricketer and publisher, coming from Williams & Norgate; Austin Harrison and Norman Douglas outside the office of *The English Review*; and authors at every twenty yards. In one morning one might see Joseph Conrad, W. H. Hudson, John Masefield, Hall Caine, Israel Zangwill, H. G. Wells, and D. H. Lawrence. Zangwill and Hall Caine, callous to the suffering they might cause to the editor of *The Tailor and Cutter*, maintained the tradition of dress by which one could recognise an author on sight. The others affected the modern, self-obscuring style.

Henrietta Street and its neighbours have still, in the main, a literary atmosphere, but of late years publishers have shown a tendency to scatter. One finds them now in all parts of London. Paternoster Row, though now rather more drapery than literary, still houses some dozen. Others one finds in the Adelphi, in Bloomsbury; a few in Mayfair; a few in Soho; and one at least as far out as South Kensington.

If one's interest was in the theatre, Bedford Street, which adjoins Henrietta Street, afforded an amusing pageant. The Yorick Club was there and the Bodega was there. The Bodega, still there, made quite a figure in the theatrical and literary life of those days. It was there that Robert Sherard found Ernest Dowson at almost his last gasp. It was there that Joseph Conrad and Stephen Crane had their first long talk. There you could meet three or four hundred old actors, each of whom, it seemed, had played Second Grave-digger to Irving. There, on Saturday noons, you could see most of the lions who were appearing at the Tivoli matinee. They made a group of their own, distinct from the actors; a Bohemia within a Bohemia. Few of these distinctive rendezvous remain to-day. Once upon a time those in a particular walk of life seemed to find delight in getting together. Now they seem anxious to get apart. They live as far from each other as possible, and if they join a club it is often not a club frequented by their profession. They no longer live in enclosed worlds of "shop." They scatter and penetrate to as many other worlds as possible. The old colonies have broken up, and scarcely any district of London now retains any fixed residential note. Where one does find a group with a regular meeting-place, it is composed usually of students or mere dilettanti of the arts. The chief cause for this is the car, which enables people to live some way out, and at week-ends to escape all town concerns and flee to the hills. Forty years ago escape was not so facile, and men tied to town over week-ends were driven to gather in confraternities.

Time and changing mode, besides carrying away the "character," have carried away many other once-common sights of the streets. Street entertainment, though it still exists in the form of Welsh miners singing choruses, ex-Service men playing jazz, and acrobats performing to theatre queues, is no longer so rich and varied as it was. You could once find some form of public amusement at every half-mile, and every suburban High Street on a Saturday night was a mixture of market and music-hall. At one point you would find a Highlander (probably from Camden Town) with bagpipes, and a lady partner doing the sword dance. A few yards away a man and woman doing a thought-reading act. Then a trained horse spelling "corn" and "hay" from lettered cards. Then a peep-show of a village street which sprang into activity if you put a penny in the slot. Then a preacher calling you to repentance. Then a one-man band--a man who carried and worked with mouth and with different limbs, a big drum, a triangle, Pan-pipes, cymbals, and concertina. Then a contortionist and escapist being roped and manacled. Then a weight-lifter; an Italian woman with a cage of fortune-telling budgerigars; a tattooed sailor advertising a tattooist--in short, a small Batholomew Fair every Saturday night, and a gusto to it which is, or seems to be, absent even from the Bank Holiday Fairs of to-day. The naphtha torches of the stalls, the incandescent lamps of the shops, and the candles used by the performers, gave the affair a carnival note which the modern stall, with its electric fittings, cannot equal. Electric light can give brilliance, and can make a brave display, but after the naphtha torch it seems austere and thin.

Casual carnival is no longer in fashion. We still have our carnivals, but they are organised: you buy tickets for them. We have lost the habit of breaking into spontaneous street-carnival, and perhaps in the interest of order it is well we have. Yet in such casual carnival as the return from Epsom on Derby Night I do not recall much disorder. This affair was a feature of the South London year. All the young of that part of South London on the road to the downs turned out for it, and from six o'clock to ten o'clock the road from Epsom through Ewell, Morden, Merton, Tooting, Balham, Clapham and Kennington to the bridges was a madly mixed procession. Four-in-hands, with amateur whips and liveried guards sounding the post-horns; victorias, landaus, traps, dog-carts, brakes, governess-carts, donkey-carts, milk-floats--anything that went on wheels. And the whole procession moving to that spirit of deliberate insanity which used to inspire the carnivals of Nice. It was, of course, a much heavier affair than any Latin carnival, being an English affair, but it caught something of that state of the human creature who is for once what he wants to be instead of the servant of his inhibitions. Every vehicle was decorated, if not with flowers, with paper streamers, flags, ribbons. The four-in-hands, the victorias and the landaus were sufficient show in themselves, but in the humbler vehicles eccentric head-dress, eccentric costume and eccentric decoration of the horses and donkeys prevailed. A typical example of the period's idea of fun was to dress the donkey's fore-legs in a pair of lady's knickers. The travellers saluted the crowd on the pavement, and the crowd saluted the travellers. The salutations were seldom in the best of taste. Indeed, the whole humour of the thing was of a kind which this age could not tolerate. It was that crowd-humour of London which Chaucer knew and Shakespeare knew, and which persisted until general education brought self-consciousness and better deportment. It took to its bed after Mafeking Night, and the general use of the car gave it its final despatch.

Another mortality is the street-cry. Of all the picturesque vendors, each with his peculiar chant, who gave colour to the streets, we have now only the lavender-woman and the muffin-man. But when I recall my childhood, and the blurred streets of those days, I hear the cry of the salt-man who, with donkey and barrow, hawked salt which he cut as required from one large block. I hear the last faltering accents of the penny pie-man. I hear the sweep's mournful herald of his presence, and the coal-man was heard "with cadence deep" in my day as in Dean Swift's day. The milk-woman, carrying her cans on a yoke, could be heard with her "Mee-yul-koo," and one of the terrors of my young life was an unseen creature which went through the October twilight, chanting to a down-scale tune: *"Old Moore's Almanack, Old Moore's Almanack."* I did not hear what he was chanting; I heard only the accent, which seemed charged with all the woe and mystery of London. He was one of the ravens of the night, of which the other was a fearful voice, not now permitted to scare wakeful children; the voice of the newsboy, with his "'Nother horrible mur-der by the Rip-per. . . . Pa-per." And there were the "Chairs to Mend" woman, the "Hot Rolls" boy, the Sarsaparilla hawker, the cats'-meat man, the rag-boddler-bone man (with balloons and flag) and the geranium merchant--"three pots a shilling." But unless you lived in a suburb you won't know anything about those mysteries. And you won't know, or care, why the baked-potato man has disappeared, or what has happened to the Italian with his pedestal organ and his monkey, or why the changing mode needed to have changed so violently as to rob you of hot rolls, and balloons and flags.

I spoke earlier of the disappearance of the Cockney slang and its replacement by American slang. Equally notable, at this day, is the disappearance of the Cockney himself. A fourth generation of the London-born is hard to find. The coster, of course, threw away his distinctive clothes and deportment as soon as Albert Chevalier brought him to public view on the music-hall stage. So, later, did the navvy, as you will discover if you have the hunt I had for corduroy trousers for the garden. And now the Cockney seems to have been exterminated, or to have hidden himself so successfully that there is no tracing him. I believe he must be about somewhere in the city, but the evidence is meagre. What song the sirens sang, or what name Achilles assumed among women, are not greater mysteries than the hiding-place of the Londoner in London.

I have met Londoners keeping seaside hotels, Londoners keeping lemonade stalls in the middle of Dartmoor, Londoners driving buses in Cumberland, Londoners in the Welsh hills, and Londoners working in Paris, Brussels, Amsterdam, Cannes and Nice. But to find them in London . . . You may lunch at one of London's best-known grill-rooms. The scene is assumed by strangers to be typical of London and London life. Actually it is typical only of the provinces. It is filled with a company connected with London and commonly associated with London--famous actors, actresses, famous musicians, social leaders, authors--all part of the London scene and leading their lives in London; and not one of them a Londoner. The born Londoner can spot his fellow or the man from outside without seeing his face or hearing his voice. He need only see him walk across the room, or shake hands; he need only see the back of his neck or the set of his shoulders, and he knows him for Londoner or provincial. Over there a man who has written many novels about London and is known as a London novelist. Every line of his body carries the marks of the shires. Next him is a Cockney comedian whose ears and neck proclaim his Midland origin. Elsewhere is a "well-known man about town," whose very walk announces him as Devonshire; a man to whom London means nothing but a "season" with its hub at Hyde Park, and who knows less about the intimate London than a Northumbrian who has a cousin living in Bloomsbury.

You may go to Fleet Street and look among the men who produce in London the daily record of London's life. You will see many Scots, numbers of Welshmen and Irishmen, and men from the northern shires. But if there is a Londoner at work among them he has closely disguised himself. You may go to cheap tea-shops at busy hours. A stranger, observing the customers, would think "Here, at any rate, is typical London." But let him talk to the people, and he will find that this one came from Hampshire last year, that one's home is in Nottingham, and another came from Shropshire two years ago, and the family of another moved in from Norfolk twelve years ago. You may go to Brixton Road, where, if anywhere, you should find true London. You talk to the shop-keepers. This one came from Southampton, the other from Cardiff, another from Colchester. Try Camden Town. Talk to the stall-keepers, who look as Cockney as any figure drawn by a comic artist to represent the Cockney. This one is a gipsy, the other from Suffolk, another from Berkshire. Wherever you go, you find that the "typical London crowd" is composed mainly of people who were born far from London. After ten or fifteen years they call themselves Londoners but on challenge they collapse to Birmingham or Liverpool or Leeds.

It is the same all over the seven hundred square miles. Scratch a self-styled Londoner and you find a provincial. London has a bad name for crime, while actually the Londoner is a good law-abiding fellow. I doubt if twenty per cent. of London crime can be traced to true Londoners; the bulk of it is the work of these expatriated provincials. They have taken London. They have taken our restaurants, our bars and our clubs. They have taken the best jobs. They have given themselves the leading rôles on the London stage. They have pushed the Londoner right off the main streets, and compelled him to retire to the back streets. I don't complain of the success of their drive; the Londoner has allowed it, and deserves his defeat by his quiescence. But if Government protects me from the cheap and good produce of men who live in foreign countries, why can't the L.C.C. protect me from the competition of people who belong to foreign *counties* and who invade my territory and seize the best things in it? If a musician who speaks Italian is barred from England because English musicians are out of work, why should a musician who speaks Yorkshire be allowed to work in London when London musicians are out of work. Or why should a Devonshire entertainer be allowed to practise in Surrey? Why can't we have London for the Londoners, and an immigration fee of say, a hundred guineas from all provincials who wish to become Londoners? Or plates of poisoned tripe at the northern railway termini and poisoned pasties at the southern?

In another sphere the Londoner has allowed himself to be pushed into the background by the provincial. Think of all the novels of London life which are accepted in the country as authoritative. How many of them were written by Londoners? Not one in fifty. The "regional" novel has been for the last century or so a notable feature of English fiction, but all the novels of this kind which survive have been the work of natives of those regions. No immigrant could have written the Wessex novels of Hardy or the Warwickshire novels of George Eliot; the Shropshire novels of Mary Webb or the East Anglian novels of R. H. Mottram. Yet the bulk of the "London" novels, which the provincials accept as we accept the rural, have been written by immigrants. The outstanding novelist of London life came from Portsea. Thackeray came from India, but came at so early an age that perhaps one may stretch a point and allow him as a Londoner. But one cannot make this allowance to the others who have been identified with the interpretation of London and London life: they did not settle in town until early manhood. We have Walter Besant, from Portsmouth; George Gissing, from Wakefield; Arnold Bennett, from the Potteries; Jerome K. Jerome, from Walsall; Pett Ridge, from Kent; Michael Arlen, from Lancashire; J. B. Priestley, from Yorkshire; Thomas Moult, from Derbyshire. All of them accepted as "London" novelists. To-day we have among us only one "London" novelist who is a Londoner. That is Mr. Frank Swinnerton.

How this has happened I do not know, for London is not without its great names in literature. But they have turned, oddly enough, not to the novel, but to poetry. And even in poetry they have used none of the swarming themes which London life affords. There seems to have been a mutual change-over. The country people rushed into London to write novels about London life; the London-born poets rushed into the country to write pastorals. They make a noble company--Chaucer, Spenser, Herrick, Crashaw, Dekker, Ben Jonson, Milton, Gray, Pope, Blake, Keats, Byron, Hood, Browning and Rossetti; yet, London-born as they were, not one of them wrote a "London" poem. All of them tuned their lyres to the country key; even Herrick, who loathed the country life of which he sang with such a golden note. No Londoner, as I say, could, after a few years in Yorkshire or Somerset, produce a Yorkshire or Somerset novel which would satisfy the natives of Yorkshire or Somerset that he knew what he was writing about and had got their inwardness in his bones. But these provincial immigrants can produce their "London" novels without challenge, despite their deplorable contortions when they present a London character talking what they think is Cockney. If a Londoner, writing a Potteries novel, made the characters begin their sentences with "Iss fay" and "Look you, indeed," he would be making no greater break than some of these authors make with their attempts at Cockney dialect. But they get away with it and are accepted, and perhaps the explanation is that London is not a "region" in the sense that the West Riding or East Anglia or Dorset is a "region." It has no permanent soil, no unchanging background, no rooted life that can be absorbed only through the bones and the blood. The Cockney will not "stay put" as rural families do, and consequently London is always fluid. It is a fusion of all elements of English life, and any man from any part of England can find his place in it. It will accept him and open to him. The country is more reticent. It gives itself only to its sons, and when the Cockney goes to make his home in it he has to wrestle with it. Perhaps that is where he has gone and why the country districts are in such a sad state. I don't know. I only know that he is not easily located in London these days.

I think the "character" whose disappearance from the London scene I most regret is that character which was so popular that at various times it was given affectionate nick-names. I mean the golden sovereign. For with the disappearance of that pleasing trifle came a complete change in the price of things. Apart from the fact that pieces of printed paper do not give you the feeling of being rich--however many you may carry with you--you can buy so little with them. The sovereign looked like riches and was. His potentialities were vast. His very gleam gave promise of good things and many of them. His weight reassured you. Often in hard times he was a widow's cruse. He might be the last you possessed, but while you could feel him in your pocket he lent you a confidence which your last five-pound note never lends. I have sometimes told young men what I have done in a London evening with one sovereign, and they look at me and look at each other, silently remarking that the old man's memory's going. But it isn't.

Often and often, in the years just before the war, a friend and myself have met at six o'clock, possessing a sovereign each. We have had aperitifs. We have dined in Soho at one of the places which soared beyond the general run of one-and-sixpence by serving a half-crown or three-shilling dinner--five courses, including game, and very good, though not Lucullan. We have had a bottle, often a bottle and a half, of reasonable claret, or flasks of Chianti, and have finished dinner with a liqueur. We have taken a cab to a theatre. We have bought seats in the dress-circle. We have taken a cab from the theatre to the station. At the station we have had a parting drink or so. And always, even if we had gone to a Caruso and Melba night at Covent Garden (gallery 2s. 6d.) we got home with some loose change. Indeed, we have often had amusing evenings when we had only five or six shillings each. On those hard-up occasions, the half-crown dinner was beyond us. We went instead to the Dieppe, the Franco-Suisse, or one of the many other places which did a four-course bourgeois dinner for one shilling. A bottle of *ordinaire* was a shilling; in some places tenpence. In these smaller places any of the usual liqueurs was sixpence. The ordinary brands of cigarette were threepence for ten, and good Turkish were sixpence for ten. One shilling would admit you to the Promenade Concerts or to the pit of a music-hall, which mostly had a bill of sixteen or eighteen turns, twelve of them "stars." After the show you could get a bottle of beer of one of the famous brands for threepence, or a proprietary whisky for fourpence. And even if you had two or three you still would not, at the end of the evening, have spent six shillings.

That is what poor young men could get in those days. The well-to-do must have had real trouble in spending their money, for even in the best restaurants five pounds went somewhat laggingly. The duty on wine was then much lower, and though the best restaurants put the best price on wines which were cheaper in the smaller places, they were still asking the sort of price now asked by second- and third-rate places. I have just looked at a wine-list of 1912. In it I find a Dow's port of 1884, at eighty-eight shillings a dozen; a Clos de Vougeot of 1894, at sixty-three shillings a dozen; a Château Lafite of 1890, at forty shillings a dozen; and of the Moselles, the princesses of the wine realm, a Berncastler Doktor of 1907 at fifty-eight shillings a dozen. Prices which one now pays for ordinary table wines.

Almost anything you wanted could be got then at a price which to-day purchases only the commonplace. To qualify as a spendthrift you must have had to think hard. One of "Pitcher's" stories about Phil May illustrates this. Phil May had attended the National Sporting Club, and had backed a lad who was not thought to have a chance. His lad won, and Phil May drew thirty pounds. Being Phil May, he saw no purpose in taking that thirty pounds home. It must be spent. It was then half-past eleven, but it must be spent. He invited all the people round about to come and have supper with him. He took them in cabs to a restaurant. He ordered a light but (as he thought) expensive supper, and kept the wine-waiter busy. Five or six friends had followed him as guests, but half-way through the meal he noted with some dismay that they were drinking very little, and that few bottles were being opened. This would not do: the thirty pounds must be spent. He called the waiter, and announced that he would like to finish the meal with a *fresh* fruit salad, and liqueur dressing. The waiter demurred and called the head-waiter. The head-waiter said that it *could* be done, but did Mr. May remember that it was January and that fresh strawberries, cherries, peaches, were likely to be--"Make the salad," said May. After some furious rushing around Covent Garden by the Kitchen Staff, the salad appeared; a magnificent bowl of out-of-season fruits. It was eaten and approved. The bill came. Phil May looked at it; then threw it down with a "Damn!" Even with the salad he hadn't spent his thirty pounds.

Phil May was a good specimen of the London "character," though he was really an immigrant from Leeds. Stories about him are innumerable. I can think of nobody to-day whose personality so constantly gives rise to anecdote and legend, and I can see none coming from the young. Nobody eagerly approaches you to tell you the "latest" about So-and-so, as I have heard they did with the "latest" about Phil May and Whistler and a few others of that period. We have our geniuses, but they do not claim their right to full *being*. There is no "latest" to be told. They seem, as I have said, only anxious to show that they are as sensible as merchants and as conventional as lawyers; as, at root, true genius always is. But genius has a licence to permit its little devils to play in public, while commercial men and lawyers dare not display their little devils outside the privacy of their own set. It is odd that modern genius ignores this licence. I recall from thirty years ago a music-hall song which petulantly inquired: "*Must* you have beef with your mustard?" We have the beef to-day in our geniuses. I wish they would bring with them a dash of mustard and give us a touch of the old fire of character.

Apart from individual characters, whole types of character have merged themselves in the common stock. Just as the London man has suffered from the craze for standardisation, so has the London girl. She is always, of course, under a fire of criticism concerning her behaviour and her dress and her masculine activity, but that comes mainly from prejudiced elders. We all, I suppose, fix our ideal of girlhood on the girls we knew in our teens. Men who were seventeen or eighteen in the forties of last century had nothing good to say of the hoyden of 1870, and those who were seventeen or eighteen in the sixties remembered girls of the "Alice" sort and looked askance at the fast miss of 1900; while those who were youths in 1900, though they have more tolerance than their fathers and grandfathers, and are prepared to approve the young thing of 1934, still see the ideal girl as a girl with flowing curls, and untroubled profile, and calm blue eyes. In most matters the modern London girl is an improvement on her elders, and notably in her absence of feminine humbug. She is direct, self-reliant, and honest in her attitudes. She knows more, and her mind is quicker. Forty years ago most girls were "dumb," and nobody thought of giving them that label. To-day that condition is the exception, and a word had to be found for it.

The only criticism I would make of her is that she is too much of a muchness. In my youth all girls were different. Prettiness was the standard then, where piquancy is the standard to-day. But it was a prettiness in variety. A dozen girls in a room were a dozen distinct girls. To-day, you may talk separately to a dozen girls in a room and all the time feel that you are talking to the same girl. Among the well-to-do classes particularly, the girl in face and figure is a stereo of all other girls: thin face, slim hips, slim fingers, and standardised expression. And in the street it is difficult to guess at a glance, save from the quality of her clothes, where she belongs. In the past you could immediately recognise the social girl, the middle-class girl, the City girl and the factory-girl. Each had its own tone, its own dress, and its own bearing. The factory-girl wore a black straw hat, ear-rings, a "Mizpah" brooch, and hair dressed in rolls over her ears. The City girl was neat and severe. The middle-class girl was also neat, but added a touch of the style and chic which in those days could only be had by money. The Society girl was consciously and demonstrably the Society girl. In these times, while the higher and the lower ranks are still distinguishable, the intermediate rank, and all the little ranks within it, have fused, and only fine and closely-observed shades mark the difference between the shop-assistant and the actress, or the young girl of Mayfair and the young girl of Hampstead.

The credit for this sameness, if it is a credit, must go to that bold and ardent portent of the nineties--the New Woman. It was she, in her Trilby hat and bloomers and tweed jacket and collar, who opened the world to the young girl of to-day. It was she who blazed the trail for Votes for Women, for entrance to all professions until then reserved to men, for mixed bathing, for sun-bathing, for tennis shorts, for bachelor flatlets and--for uniformity. She was the Woman Who Did, and she did well in all these things, save the last. When John Knox wrote of "this monstrous regiment of women," he can hardly have guessed how accurate the word regiment would be, centuries later. Women and girls have won their freedom, thanks to the New Woman, but, having won it, they seem unable to use it. After running about for a while, and tasting it, the next thing they did was to enter a new servitude and make themselves look as much like each other as possible. To-day there are neither pretty girls nor plain girls; everywhere you see the same keen features and alert eyes; the same scarlet lips and scarlet finger-nails; the same poise, the same rather arctic charm, and the same funny little hat. They are the progeny of the New Woman--a regiment of Good Sorts.

As the coster and the navvy have changed their costume and their deportment, so have less agreeable types. In my childhood there was much talk of a certain figure of the rougher quarters called the "hooligan." He was recognisable on sight. To-day he is not to be seen. He went out at the same time as the roaring, round-the-town boys of the West End. He was a lower example of their sort, a figure of an age, a smasher of things for the sake of smashing things. When life became more severe, and expenditure of energy had to have some purpose, he ceased to be, and his place was taken by neatly-tailored young men who do not break idly into disorder. They break with purpose and with method, and with fast cars. They are the smash-and-grab men and the hold-up men. You might sit with them in trains and buses and restaurants, and never know them from book-keepers and respectable householders. The hooligan had a contemporary, a more serious and business-like fellow, but equally recognisable. He, too--Burglar Bill--has ceased to dress his part and announce his calling to the world. He appears now as the cat-burglar, and often doubles the part by posing as a young man about town. He frequents West End bars and restaurants, and often is found to be mixing with reputable people. Just as many of the pleasures and conveniences once restricted to the rich can now be had by the people, so many of the activities once restricted to the poor have been taken over by the educated whose education has unfitted them for the new intellectual demands of the professions or the far-sighted enterprise of modern commerce.

Another type for which you will look in vain is that figure who, up to 1914, was so common that at various periods he had a stock name. At one time he was a Swell; then a Johnny; then a Masher; then a Blood; and his last manifestation was the K'nut. The nearest figure we now have to him is the gigolo, but there is a great gulf between the demeanour and operations of the two types. The Gay Old Boy, too, once a familiar figure of the West End, has gone, and his Lady Friend cannot easily be found. These types, I think, went out when the Empire Promenade went out and when Leicester Square suffered an overhaul, and lost those cosmopolitan bars which were the rendezvous of the Pretty Ladies. The Johnny, the Gay Old Boy, and the Lady Friend were part of the furniture of Leicester Square, as you may see from the pictures of the black-and-white artists of the period. With the passing of the Leicester Square legend they also passed. Outside London, however, the legend seems to survive. Young provincials, I notice, and visitors from the Dominions still want to see Leicester Square. This may be due to its being enshrined in old songs; but though these songs carried its legend into all sorts of remote villages, it was not, I think, the songs that set it on the map, nor anything that it possessed in itself. It owes most of its fame, I fancy, to Mrs. Ormiston Chant. Until she arrived, nobody, not even frequenters or casual visitors, realised what a depraved spot it was. It was from her that it had its best time. About ten years later, in the early nineteen-noughts, it began to flag. The music-halls, who had been its major celebrants, suddenly turned on their old favourite, and the late George Formby hastened the end of that particular phase of its life with his songs ridiculing the new kind of youth about town--"It's My Night Out," "I'm One of The Boys" and "We All Went to Leicester Square." The funeral hymn of its raffish phase was sung by the soldiers when they chose "Tipperary" for their marching song. In that song the author wrote better than he knew. "Good-bye, Piccadilly; farewell, Leicester Square." It was an adieu to an age. Piccadilly and Leicester Square survive, as bright as ever they were; but the self-conscious gaiety and that note which caused music-hall comedians to smirk when they mentioned them, are gone. To-day, Leicester Square is clean and lively, and on a Spring morning it is one of the most pleasant spots of the town. Entertainment is there, but of a fresher, more sensible kind, and people of all sorts frequent it at all hours of day and night. It is within my not-too-aged recollection that at one time women alone at night went some way round to avoid passing through it.

In place of the old type of lounge, in which women only of a "certain type" were seen, we have the hotel lounge. As America has captured our entertainment industry, and taken the marrow out of our colloquial talk and substituted trans-Atlantic zest, so it has imposed upon us the American feature of the hotel lounge, which in every American town is everybody's rendezvous. It can be, and is, put to many uses. People sit in it, and stand in it, and think in it, and walk in it, and meet their friends, or day-dream in it. There seems to be only one thing people don't do in a hotel lounge. They may sit, but they don't lounge. Only once have I seen a man actually lounging in the lounge, with all his limbs at disorderly ease; and it turned out that he was drunk, and the staff quickly stopped him from using the place in accord with its name. There should be some new word for it, since an hour in a lounge is anything but an hour of ease; it is more like an hour in a maelstrom.

Spend an hour in the lounge of one of the new popular hotels. From half-past ten in the morning until midnight it is in such a stir that for all the lounging you can do you might as well be in the middle of Cheapside. In the morning and afternoon it is occupied mainly by tourists and by women from the suburbs and provinces taking refreshment between spells of shopping, or meeting their friends. In the evening the company is diversified--clergymen and small business men; young people of all kinds; foreign students and wanderers for whom there is no label. The lounge lizard is neither so numerous nor so highly developed in England as in America, though if America will give us time we may be able to produce it as a successor to the Johnnies, the Mashers and the K'nuts. What we already possess is what I may call the Lounge Lizzie. She is not the housewife taking an hour's rest between shoppings. She is a quiet, respectable woman--and lonely. She appears to have no shopping to do, no work to do, nothing to do, and very little money. She sits in these places hour by hour, sipping coffee and wearing in her eyes the guilty look of one engaged in the dreary business of getting through life without living. The business is called Killing Time, and I think the hotel lounges of Europe and America have seen more of this kind of moral murder than any other enclosed places.

These lounges make a strong appeal to those living in cramped villas on cramped incomes. They are in the topographical centre of things. They are spacious and lofty. They are furnished like a private drawing-room imagined by a film-producer. They give to tired people a reflection of the world which they taste vicariously in novels and in movies: a Monte Carlo world which, in their view, is Life. They appease a modern appetite. They give colour and movement, and a tonic sense of affluence and ease, to millions who have never before had a share of them, and this reacts pleasantly upon the general social tenor and outlook.

In Victorian days, when places were built for the use of the people, nobody thought of making them gorgeous replicas of palaces. As little as possible was spent on them, and the promoters went on wondering why they failed. Then some bright spirit came along with the idea of building the kind of place that had formerly been built for the well-to-do, and of making the same charges that were made in the old dingy places. I can hear the comments of the prophets, who, like so many prophets, were thinking thirty years behind their time. "Hopeless. He'll never get his money back. How could he--with all that outlay and those ridiculous prices?" They forgot the simple economic fact that twenty shillings are the same as one pound; that three thousand people bringing in a shilling every day are as good as one hundred and fifty people bringing in a pound. More certain, too; since there are millions from whom the place can draw its three thousand, and not so many from whom it can draw its hundred and fifty. Mr. Woolworth's success is due to his discovery of the fact that millions of people can spend sixpence at five different times, or threepence at ten different times, who never at any time have half-a-crown to spend. It is irritating to be faced with proof of a proverb which you don't like and never believed; but these people have proved that if you look after the pence, the pounds will look after themselves.

The doubting attitude of the business-man-prophet recalls a story I read recently in a book of London gossip published in the late nineties. It was the recollections, mainly of clubs and taverns, of Edward Callow, who at that date could look back to London life in the eighteen-forties. The story concerns the time when there were no Charing Cross Station and no Charing Cross Hotel. In the Haymarket of those days there stood, where His Majesty's and the Carlton now stand, the Italian Opera House, still remembered in the Opera Arcade, running from Charles Street to Pall Mall. The Charles Street side of this block was occupied by a small hotel which, some time during the sixties, was wound-up and put on the market. The author and a few of his City friends formed a plan for purchasing the hotel, and with it all other interests in the whole block, and erecting upon the site the kind of hotel which is now the prevailing London hotel--namely, a huge American hotel. The plan went well. Many important people became interested in the project, as directors, and an advisory board of men with long experience of hotel management was formed. Plans and estimates were drawn up, and all arrangements made for the purchase of existing leases. Then, at one of the board meetings of the new company, it was announced that the South Eastern Railway had lodged plans for the erection of a large hotel at their new terminus at Charing Cross. Whereupon the advisory board of the proposed large hotel on the Haymarket site, the men experienced in the hotel business, gave advice to their directors as follows: That it was useless for them to proceed with their project, since London *could not possibly support two such hotels*. A few years later, as the author, with just bitterness, remarks, this advisory board had before their eyes Northumberland Avenue and its hotels.

Another type who was regarded at the beginning of the century as a permanent feature of London life, and is now in retirement, is the old horse-bus driver. The motor-bus driver of to-day is a fine type, and performs an exacting job with unusual skill and suave temper. But one does not know much about him. The horse-bus driver was in touch with his front-seat passengers, and they could talk to him. Londoners then were not oversensitive to wind and rain, and the open top of the bus gave them a view of the world through which they rumbled, and inspired that casual conversation which open air always inspires among strangers, and which enclosed places always stifle. In sunshine or pouring rain the mere presence of the driver, and perhaps the presence of the horses, was an incentive to talk; but on the motor-bus, whether covered or open, the driver is set apart from his passengers. There is no chance of talking to him, and he goes so swiftly through the streets and makes such brief pauses that there is little chance even of observing him. In the past, men who lived in the suburbs and went every day to the City got to know their bus-driver, and their front seat was always reserved for them. If they were not at the corner when their bus stopped, the bus would wait for them. On the way to town they would discuss the news and the outlook with the driver. He made a faint link with the old coachmen whom the railways had expelled from the roads of England. He had their weather-beaten face, their independence, their stolidity. At times he was gruff, but he was seldom morose. When he, in his turn, was expelled from the roads of London, the public, which had taken him for granted, began to miss him. It even got sentimental about him, as it does about ordinary things which have ceased to be, and attributed to him many qualities which he did not possess.

One of these was wit. Older people began to tell each other about the witty bus-drivers they had known, and to recall examples of their salt. Within my own experience I am unable to confirm this *ana*. I was going about London for twelve years before the horse-bus left the streets, and was keeping my ears and eyes open, and not once did I encounter a flash of wit. Not once did I hear those drivers or conductors say anything of original spirit. What I did hear, and often, was constant echo of the latest music-hall gag. I may have been merely unlucky, but I believe that was all that anybody heard. A fair specimen could be heard when a horse-bus was passing one of the early motor-buses which had broken down--as they frequently did. "Hi--why donya sit on his head, mate?" The uneducated Cockney is not truly a wit. Where he does shine, and where he is richly characteristic of a great city, is in truculence and invective.

"Wodger mean, gin me that nasty look?"

"Oo--me? I-ne-geeya no nasty look."

"Su did."

"Ono I din. Yad it fore I sawya."

As no city can so abash the hero who sets out to conquer it in a week as London, so no man can wither and blast the pompous as the Londoner. But not with wit; with well-frozen scorn. And the Cockney girl is perhaps even better at it than the Cockney lad.

Around 1906-7 we could travel about London by the new vehicles or the old. We could make part of our journey by horse-bus and continue it by venturing on a Vanguard, an Arrow, or a Rapide. We could go to the theatre by hansom and return home by taxi. At that time the sway of the battle was not clearly indicated, and taxis and motor-buses were impertinent intruders among the horse-traffic, which pronounced upon them such bitter comment as is to-day pronounced upon what remains of the horse-traffic. By 1909 the issue was clear. The horse must go. By 1911 so far as buses were concerned, it had gone. It was in that year that the last horse-bus made its last over-the-bridge journey. For a few years more the hansom kept up a sort of guerilla warfare with the taxi, and up to 1918 it was not such a rarity on the streets as to be pointed out and looked at. But its day in London, and the horse's day, was done, and since the end of the war street-orderlies, lads who ran in and out of the traffic with pan and brush, have had little to do. Our main streets, which, since the beginning of London, had held the smell of the stable, were thenceforth to hold the reek of petrol. The taxi and the motor-bus were fixed, and will remain fixed until those plans for aerodromes and landing-stages in the centre of London become facts, and change yet again the face and tone of the London scene.

We have little chance, as I say, of knowing the motor-bus driver and comparing him in personality with the horse-bus driver. But the taxi-driver we can exchange words with, and get to know, and in comparing him with the hansom cabby of yesterday I think the balance falls in his favour. He and the motor-bus driver, I believe, are officially recognised as the most skilled and considerate of road-users. Foreign visitors to London talk so much and so often of the courtesy and efficiency of our police that one might think they had never noticed our other public servants. Could they not spare the blushes of the police for awhile, and give a nod of recognition elsewhere? Could they not tell us sometimes that our telephone operators sure know their stuff, that our postmen have gotten the world beat for snappy delivery, or that our taxi-drivers are--how you say?--zo zweet, *n'est-ce pas?* Like the contemporaries of the horse-bus driver, we too much take the taxi-driver for granted, and if we talk of him at all we talk of his faults. Only when he is gone shall we get sentimental about him and recall his peculiar flavour.

How many times, when I have been lost in wildernesses, has he picked me up and returned me to civilisation. When a storm has caught me in a lonely street without an overcoat he has appeared at the corner and rescued me. When I have had to keep an appointment at a club whose address I did not know he has delivered me there. When I have, on two occasions, stopped him and said "Nearest doctor" he has found him. And when, as happens to the best of us, I have had no money for his tip, and have told him so, he has not cursed me. "That's all right, sir. Another time, perhaps." Much of the vague hostility towards him seems to centre on this matter of tipping, but I have always found that if you frankly tell him you are short, he will accept the explanation civilly. To neglect this explanation, and to hand over the exact fare without a word, does sometimes lead to hard feeling. His economic position is by no means the bed of roses many people think it to be, and considering the hours he works, and that his best work is done in foul weather, his rough-and-ready good manners and his level civility are to be applauded.

He seldom bursts into spring-tide smiles, and is not much given to joking. This is because he has to be alert not only for his job itself, but for many external details. He has to be on his guard against those who consider him an easy mark--the bilkers, and those who want to treat him as taxi-man, porter, footman, banker and street-guide. His only job is driving a taxi, and he need perform no other service; though for people who behave decently he often will. He will almost always help with the luggage if you *ask* him; he will oblige a request where he is within his rights in ignoring a command; and his knowledge of London is usually available to any inquirer, whether his taxi is wanted or not. If you have run short of money, and can prove where you live, he will drive you anywhere and call for his fare next day; and I have met many instances of his kindness to really poor people.

Anybody who has had a year's experience of Paris taxi-men ought, I think, on meeting the London taxi-man to give him a benediction. You know how it is in Paris. You take your taxi and name a street. If it isn't a main street, the driver asks you where it is and how to get to it. If you don't know, out comes his Map and

Guide. I fancy that any London taxi-man who was driven to consult a Map and Guide would either commit hara-kiri or be despatched by his colleagues. His knowledge of London is unassailable. Never have I known him hesitate, unless, that is, the street you want is an obscure street in a distant suburb. In the mad pride of my own knowledge of London I have sometimes put some pretty problems to him, but I have never puzzled him. I have taken a taxi in Coldharbour Lane and said "Percy Circus," and the man has nodded and landed me there. I have taken a taxi from a rank in Lewisham and said "Goldsmiths' Hall," and have been asked no question. I have tried the old trick of Trafalgar Square, but have never won. Always the man has come back with "Charing Cross, Chelsea, or Stepney?" I have tried to catch him taking a longer route than was necessary, but have never succeeded. There have been times when I have thought with impish delight that I had got him. "He's going the wrong way. He doesn't know. At last I can tell a taxi-man something." Then a sudden turn has brought us into a familiar street, and has taught me a quick way I didn't know. Sometimes I have been so sure that he was using too long a route that I have stopped him and challenged him. Always I have been crushed. "I know all about that. But the road's up in Euston Road. Take ten minutes getting through there."

Just as the coachmen of the early nineteenth century received their celebration in social history, and, later, the railway men received theirs, and the hansom cabbies received theirs, so, in time to come, will the motor-bus driver and the taxi-man receive theirs. I am sure it will be an affectionate celebration. The aerobus pilot we have yet to know in London, but we may be confident that when he does arrive he will be as efficient and as quietly cheerful as all other public figures of London's daily life.

SHOPS

My earliest impressions of London were, as I say, of lamps and shop-windows. The city seemed to me to be all shops: hundreds, thousands, millions of shops, every one of them an invitation, so that one was worried as to which to accept and which to pass. The shops of the little side-streets made as keen an appeal as those of the great streets. Each was an Aladdin's Cave, its windows only hinting at richer wonders awaiting those entitled to explore its dim recesses. Sometimes I was grieved to think that however zealously I set about it I would never, could never, look in the windows of every shop in London.

Among the first shops I ever saw was one whose window, at this moment of writing, is dressed as it was when I saw it from a height of three feet. While so many old-established businesses in one particular line have, in the past thirty or forty years, demolished their premises and returned to life as general stores, or at any rate six sizes larger, this shop has neither altered nor extended itself, nor even changed its style of display. It stands to-day as it did, and its windows have suffered the ferment of the years without ageing and without apeing the frantic young. It makes no concessions to those "times" which are often responsible for disastrous experiment. It has no need to. London can rush ahead or pull itself about as it pleases; this shop remains static and shows that window-dressing of the old sort can attract as many eyes as the most Picasso or Matisse challenge. It is pleasant in a world of change to find something which is at once an immovable object and an irresistible force, and I can never pass along Oxford Street without pausing at the old, familiar windows of Buszard's.

Their window-dressing may have changed in a minor point here and there, but to my eye they are the very windows of my childhood, holding the same number of tiered bride-cakes of the same design and confection, the same number of Falstaffian Dundee cakes, and the same fascinating juvenilia of the cake world. The first cakes I ever tasted must have been Buszard's, for I have a very early memory of being given money and of going in and of being served with objects more lustrous than jewels--jam-puffs, cream-buns and what-not. So long have its windows remained unchanged that it is possible that my infant godson, in his middle-age, will be able to pass along Oxford Street and show them to *his* infant godson as the windows to which his godfather brought him when he was a boy.

It is not the only London shop which has sat with folded hands and looked blandly upon all the change going on around it. The West End has some dozen examples, and the City one or two, while every suburb except the up-to-the-minute suburbs keeps an odd one tucked away somewhere. When one has used up all the general programme tours of London, one might make an Old Shop Tour. Freibourg and Treyer's, in Haymarket, looks much as it must have looked when my grandfather passed it. Berry's, the wine-merchant's, and Lock's, the hatter's, both in St. James Street, have also insisted upon retaining the hues of youth and growing old in the cravats and silk waistcoats of George Brummell. There is the chemist's shop in Drury Lane, which my mother, at the age of eighty-one, recognised as having the selfsame appearance and dressing it had when she was fourteen. There is the book-shop of Ellis, in Bond Street, one of a number in that street and its by-streets which have seen no good reason for having their faces lifted to six storeys of concrete.

My early acquaintance with Buszard's arose from my Aunt Jane and her shopping expeditions. We have all, I suppose, had an Aunt Jane, and have all, once or twice at least, gone shopping with her. Remembering those expeditions, one sees what a revolution has happened in thirty years in shops and the business of shopping, and in Aunt Janes themselves. The Aunt Janes of to-day are mainly Aunt Joans or Aunt Corals or Aunt Leslies, and are a very distant strain of the breed of Aunt Jane.

Recently a schoolboy friend brought his Aunt Leslie to see me. It was long since I had seen an aunt, as such, and it was amusing to note the thirty years' difference between her and my Aunt Jane. To the middle-aged the term Aunt still carries something which evokes respect, if not awe; for in our childhood Aunts were personages. Aunt Jane was affectionate and well-disposed towards "the children," but in the manner of a benevolent headmistress. When she was visiting, it was necessary to be a little more or a little less than one's true self. She had an eye for failings; a gentle eye, perhaps, but still an eye. When she moved she rustled, as though her very dress were aware of its office in decorating so august a figure and were sh-sh-ing the surroundings into respect. "The children" to her were a lovely but alien tribe from a country beyond her borders. Her notion of amusing you was to tell you of the worm-eaten games she played when she was young; games no decent child would be caught playing. But she made up for this by the exciting packages she brought, by her "treats" to circuses and pantomimes, her postal orders on birthdays, and the shopping tours which we were allowed to share.

There was nothing of this about Aunt Leslie. Aunt Jane's first words to her nephews were--How were they getting on at school? Aunt Leslie's first words to *her* nephew were a question--why was he wriggling about there like a rheumatic eel instead of taking her coat. At five o'clock Aunt Jane always took tea. She didn't drink tea; she "took" it, with an elegant finger. Aunt Leslie said no tea for her; rather have a spot of gin and soda if that was gin she could see on that rickety table. She was at the age at which I remember Aunt Jane--fortyish; but there was no bearded and moustached "romance" in the background. She was unmarried because, running a little business with four branches, she had no time for it. Aunt Jane regarded any change of ways and habits which happened after she was twenty as unworthy of notice, or, if noticed, to be deprecated. Aunt Leslie regarded anything that didn't belong to this week as woolly and lousy. She liked things to change frequently and violently. When Aunt Jane spoke, one listened and kept silent until she had finished. One accepted, even if one didn't approve, everything she said. Aunt Leslie's nephew derided most of her views, as being three days behind the times, and more than once it appeared that they would come to blows. Three times he told her she didn't know what she was talking about, and her only answer was profanity. I tried to visualise myself saying that to my Aunt Jane, but chaos and lightning kept blurring the picture.

When Aunt Jane left us she always slipped half-crowns into the children's hands. When Aunt Leslie left my flat she stated that she was broke, and that her nephew must lend her half-a-crown for a taxi, and it was no good his saying he hadn't got it because she'd seen his mother that morning give him a pound note. Aunt Leslie, I think, could give her nephew a better "time" than Aunt Jane gave hers, though Aunt Jane tried hard enough; but while no modern nephew would welcome the gift of an Aunt Jane, there was a little something about Aunt Jane which Aunt Leslie hasn't got. She wasn't so "human" as Aunt Leslie, but she has left an aroma. She had dignity, delicacy, tenderness, and pathetic traits of that sort. At most times she was a bore, though maybe that was our fault for being bored; but when you were sick or in trouble she was magnificent. Aunt Leslie is always the good companion, and always ready to do what she can for people if it doesn't involve too much trouble; but I doubt her lasting capacity for sympathy. Still, she will probably earn her place in the heaven of Aunts. It won't be the same heaven as Aunt Jane's, which is a quiet, elegant heaven of chintz parlours and silver tea-sets. It will be a jolly heaven with golf-courses and dance-bands. And both heavens will be London, for Aunt Jane loved London in her way as much as Aunt Leslie in hers.

I do not now go shopping with women, but in walking about London and occasionally buying something, I observe the customers and the staff, and I can perceive a wide gulf between the old and the new technique of shopping. Even in the most serious of all departments of shopping, the dressmaker's studio, there is an air which--forgive the profanity--is almost snappy as compared with the rites and ceremonies of those places at the Diamond Jubilee era. When Aunt Jane entered her dressmaker's, or for that matter her chemist's, or grocer's, or florist's, she entered with the air of having come for the day. She never did spend the day there, not even at the dressmaker's, but it seemed like it. Often she got out of the chemist's, the grocer's, or the florist's, in forty-five minutes, I have known her do it in thirty. But the atmosphere of the affair in each shop was that the clock had stopped, and that she and the shopman were free to discuss until next week this matter of flowers or soap or biscuits. Women still, I suppose, take it leisurely at their costumier's and hair-dresser's, but "leisurely" is a relative term, and what passes as leisurely in 1934 would in 1897 have been thought rush. In the matter of minor purchases they are almost as brisk as men. In the time Aunt Jane took to buy a hair-net the modern women has given her favourite store the once-over and is snapping into one purchase after another. The shopman saves her the trouble of looking for bargains; he thrusts them before her in special departments. In Aunt Jane's time they had to be scented and stalked, and Aunt Jane had a nose for them. Her major expeditions were centred on the Autumn sales and the January sales, but she carried her bargain-hunting zeal into every shopping visit. It was her firm conviction that all shops existed for the purpose of swindling her. Even the sales did not satisfy her: half-price she considered an outrageous price.

Husbands of to-day often complain that their wives make a fuss about shopping. They should have seen Aunt Jane preparing for a descent on Regent Street, St. Paul's Churchyard and, occasionally, Bond Street. The week of the campaign was fixed well ahead; the route and the tactics were planned; and bundles of catalogues (quaint bibelots for us, those shop catalogues of yesteryear) were scrupulously examined. I recall being an eye-witness of many stages of the campaign, notably at Gorringe's, Peter Robinson's, Dickins and Jones, Liberty's, and "Phoebe's," where her bonnets came from.

Her way of checking any unruly outbursts on our part was to tell us what "ladies" did and did not do, though why she expected healthy boys to be patterns of English ladies I don't know. However, by close observation of her lady ways, we learned a lot. We learned how to deal with careless or casual shop-assistants, and particularly how to deal with cab-drivers. She was nervous of hansoms; they looked dangerous, and I believe she thought them a little frivolous. She would trust herself only to four-wheelers. The driver of the growler, if you remember, was inclined to be not perhaps so high-handed as the driver of the hansom, but much more surly. You should have seen Aunt Jane dealing with him. In those encounters her frailty and timidity and English-lady delicacy strangely went overboard. Many a strong, silent man was crushed by the drivers of those four-wheelers, but not Aunt Jane. The driver who questioned the sum which she handed to him--she had a fixed tip for any distance: twopence--usually, after a few seconds of speech from her, drove off. They all drove off; it was only a question whether they could stand ten seconds of it or a minute and a half. Those who stood ground longest got her ultimatum--"Another word from you and I take your number."

On these shopping campaigns she seemed to fight her way to victory by use of the mystic threat of taking people's "number." Three or four times a day, if she were impeded on her march, she would threaten to take cabmen's numbers, bus-conductors' numbers, porters' numbers, District Messengers' numbers, and there was a family rumour that she had been heard to threaten to take a policeman's number. What she was going to do with these numbers when she had "taken" them, I never discovered. I don't think she knew herself, and I never actually saw her take a number. But in her spinster wanderings about London she had found that the phrase had some runic potency of creating alarm among the lower orders and of making things easier for herself, and she used it on her shopping campaigns as ignorantly and as effectively as Ali Baba used the "Open, Sesame."

She expounded to me her attitude on these occasions by saying that it never "did" to stand any "nonsense" from these people. "Nonsense" meant for her what other people mean by business. She would stand no "nonsense" from shop-keepers or restaurateurs, or from anybody who wanted to make a living. She would stand no "nonsense" from her hotel--one of the many quiet places, now vanished, which used to stand thickly in the byways of Oxford Street. She knew that the hotel hoped to make a profit out of her visits, and she refused to be the victim of any such nonsense. She would beat them down until she reached a price for her room which she thought "fair," which usually meant that the hotel made nothing out of her. Having won that victory, she would give lavish presents to attentive chamber-maids, would feed them menthol and lavender water when they had headaches, and if they were run down would arrange holidays by the sea at her cost.

Full of sympathy for certain kinds of worker, she was merciless on the more public servants--cabmen, shop-assistants, etc. She would keep shop-assistants on hot days pulling down box after box of lace or ribbons for three-quarters of an hour, and then, if their courtesy relaxed under the strain, she would talk of "reporting" them. In these days, happily, the London shop-assistants (or store-clerks, seeing that we're all American) are manumitted souls who would soon show any Aunt Jane that they, in their turn, were not standing any "nonsense"; but at the beginning of the century the customer could unload all its pent-up bad manners on the assistant, and get away with it.

To-day, a woman can do her household shopping under one roof, but in those days the big department store for women, covering most of her personal and household requirements, was only in its infancy. Aunt Jane's shopping was therefore a business of visiting, during her week, some thirty different shops, and this meant a series of buses and four-wheelers. The buses in those days still lived in the last throes of the coaching atmosphere. Instead of cabalistic numbers and initial letters, they had names. Just as the coaches had been named Defiance, Quicksilver, Wonder, Rapid, Reliable, so the buses were The Atlas, The Favourite, The Royal Blue. Most of my early rides seem to have been associated with the Royal Blue. I forget its route, but I feel sure that it touched Piccadilly Circus, and I have memories of mounting and dismounting from it at that spot on these shopping tours. It may have touched Oxford Circus, too, since it seems that one was in the Royal Blue at a few minutes to eleven, and at eleven one was buying glories in Buszard's.

I recall visits to other "pastrycook's" besides Buszard's; it was Aunt Jane's regular custom to withdraw from the fray at mid-morning and take biscuits and a glass of "sherry wine," giving me the freedom of the pastry counter. I cannot find those pastrycooks now. Indeed, I know of but one pastrycook's of the old style remaining in London, and that one is in Jermyn Street. Unless Gunter's and Rumpelmayer's can be covered by that term. Aunt Jane would never patronise the new tea-shops, which were then opening in different parts of the town, chiefly because they were new and not of her youth. She must always find a pastrycook's. Lunch meant returning to her hotel, or looking about for one of the few restaurants to which a solitary female could go. In this matter the modern woman shopper enjoys another advantage over her mother and grandmother. Not only can she do her household and garden shopping under one roof; she can spend the day there and take lunch and tea in agreeable surroundings, without leaving it. If she cares to go elsewhere, any restaurant is open to her; she could even go to a public-house if she wished to, without incurring the suspicion, common in Aunt Jane's day, of being no better than she should be. (Though how any human creature could be anything else is a question which used to puzzle me every time I saw or heard the phrase.)

I believe it was some suburban drapery store which was the pioneer in this matter of refreshment. I think I have heard that somewhere in South London a large establishment of this sort made the experiment of setting aside one room of its premises for afternoon tea. The experiment was a success, and on the news of its success a number of central London houses followed its example, and soon extended it from afternoon tea to lunch, and finally to an all-day service. Then, of course, the giant stores arrived, with their roof-garden restaurants, their palm-lounges for tea, their rest-rooms, writing-rooms, telephone-rooms, hairdressing-rooms, exhibitions and entertainments, and all the other services of a metropolitan High Street. So that the housewife of to-day can not only cover all her domestic business in one shop, but can get for nothing the sort of Happy Day which her grandmother had when she went to the Crystal Palace.

The great store certainly has advantages over the old system of little individual shops, though, on the few occasions when I have done any shopping in one of these places, I have found that at the end of the business I have walked just as far as if I had been in the street and going from one shop to another. And really, had I been in the street, dodging from one shop to another, I would not have been so tired. I would have been able to hop into taxis or buses, and drop off at the particular shop I wanted. The stores do their best for us with lifts and soft carpets, but they have not as yet any taxis or bath-chairs to convey us from department to department. Another point in which I find them at variance from the little shops is the feeling one has of being secretly watched. In the shop there is a counter, and the goods are usually on the thither side of the counter. In the store the goods are spread openly before you, all round you, on open stands and often on the floor, in such a way that you almost feel that you are invited to Please Take One. At times you may find two or three stands without assistants, and when you want to buy something you have to wander about and search for somebody who is authorised to take the money. And while you are thus wandering with your intended purchase, you have the feeling of unseen eyes following you. Nobody minds being openly watched, but this feeling of secret watching is unpleasant. There is another side to this. If these people will display their goods in this casual way, and leave the stands without attendants, can they wonder at the temptation they offer to some poor women to Take One? They constantly complain of their losses by shop-lifting, and are constantly detecting and prosecuting poor women, when it need not happen at all. Shop-lifting doesn't happen in the small, personal shops; only in the big stores. And it wouldn't happen there if the stores saw that no stand was left without an attendant, and that their shop-detectives were open watchers in uniform. This is recognised in the outside world. The plain clothes man is useful in *detecting* the commission of crime, but the greatest *preventive* of crime is the constant presence of the uniformed constable. So, in the stores, the sight of the uniform, which meant detection, would quench any temptation.

I think I still prefer the small, personal shop, but no doubt that is because I am middle-aged. The sight and associations of our first twenty years remain with us for ever and are the standard by which we judge all innovation and development. The store is an inevitable and useful growth from the shop, but, like so many large things, it has no room for character. The flavour and aroma of those small, personal shops are outside its comprehension or attainment. The store has one large and nondescript smell, but when I think of shopping I think of each separate shop and its separate smell. There was the smell of the draper's shop; the smell of the chemist's; the smell of the grocer's; the smell of the pastrycook's--what a smell!--the smell of the oil-and-colourman's; the smell of the fruiterer's; the smell of the newsagent's; the smell of the sweetstuff shop; the smell of the furniture shop. You could range the gamut of the human nose from pungent to mawkish. With the peculiar smell went the peculiar type of proprietor or assistant. Mr. Jones, who served at the grocer's, was quite unlike Mr. Smith at the oil-and-colourman's, and Mrs. Brown who kept the sweetstuff shop was a notable divergent from the type of Mrs. Robinson who kept the newsagent's. In the large shop or store there are none of these salty distinctions. One assistant is much like another, whether serving at the chemistry counter or the lingerie counter. One felt that Mrs. Robinson had carefully decided that of all lives she desired most that of newsagent, and that Mr. Jones found himself in grocering. With these others of to-day one feels only that they decided to be shop-assistants--I mean store-clerks.

But the store and the mammoth shop have their credit entry. They are lighter, cleaner, brighter. The atmosphere is brisker. There is more space and more air to breathe. There is more display, or perhaps exhibitionism is the truer word. Window-dressing is cast in a high key, as though the flamboyant friend of Wells' Mr. Polly had dressed them. (You remember the ferocious *mêlée* resulting from that young man's ambition to do a "temperamental window.") There is less servility and more actual service. And of course, with the wider facilities for transport and trade which the last forty years have brought, there is a much more varied and fresher stock; and articles which formerly could be had only by the well-to-do are now available to the many. In these modern shops you can get to-day all the commodities of all the countries of the world, fresh and fresh. Think of something odd that you would like; something Peruvian or Hondurastian or Icelandic. It is fairly certain that some London shop has it.

I seldom enter a draper's shop in these days; not once in ten years, perhaps; but when I do, though I admire the new fabrics and the new arrangements and the rainbow colours, there is one thing I miss. One thing which used to reconcile me to otherwise dreary half-hours in those dim, poky shops, when Aunt Jane and the assistant were out on the pavement matching a ribbon by the daylight which never reached the shop. That thing was the cash-railway, by which the assistant packed the bill and the money in a wooden ball, and sent it up a spiral to an overhead track, whence it travelled across the shop and dropped off the rails on to the cashier's desk. I could have watched for many more half-hours than I did the dozens of balls whizzing along the rails from all parts of the shop, never falling off even when crossing the points, but arriving patly at the station of the cashier. And then making the return journey and dropping your change into the hands of the assistant who had served you.

In those days most personal shopping had to be done in Aunt Jane's way, travelling across the town from the glove-shop to the "mantle" shop, but to-day, while the larger shops and stores make everything easy for personal shopping, even this can be avoided by those who wish. With the spread of the telephone into small homes, a great deal of shopping for common household purposes is done by this means. And there is the C.O.D. service for everybody, and for known customers the "on approval" service. One or two popular shops in central London, I notice, have caught at the C.O.D. service in a novel way. They keep their windows lit at night, so that evening strollers can see what they are offering. On the front of the shop, for the convenience of women who do not pass that way by day, is an automatic machine which, in return for sixpence, delivers a pencil and a paper pad. The woman who sees something in the window that suits her, writes her order on the pad, with name and address, and drops it in a special letter-box. The goods are sent to her next day C.O.D., and the sixpence which she put into the machine is deducted from the price.

Looking about this modern London and comparing it with the London of 1900, one sees how deeply it has become imbued with the American principle of Bigger and Better Elephants. Everything that I recall about the

London of my boyhood was small. To-day everything seems much bigger. Usually the grown-up is surprised to find how small are the places and objects which in childhood he thought big. With London and myself, it is the reverse. The small-scale London that I knew is gone; even those places which have not expanded, such as Trafalgar Square and Piccadilly Circus, *seem* much bigger. Buses are bigger, railway-carriages are wider, trams are longer. All buildings are bigger; even bus-tickets are bigger. Newspapers are bigger; public-houses are bigger; government departments are bigger; restaurants, even those of Soho, are bigger; theatres are bigger; newsboys are older and policemen are younger. The only things that have grown smaller in these thirty years are postal orders and restaurant tables. Every shop I used to know, save Buszard's and the few others I mentioned, has grown to five and six times its original stature and bulk; and banks, which used to present the appearance of being the resort of bearded misers, are now sometimes mistaken by strangers for tea-shops or movie-palaces. Even the august dress-makers of the Hanover Square region have larger premises, and no longer hide behind discreet curtains and demand three knocks and a password before admitting the stranger.

In yet another direction London's shops have shed their former selves and come out in new array. When in my childhood you went to the chemist, you found that he had nothing to sell but drugs and toilet articles. When you went to the tobacconist, you found that he sold tobacco in various forms; nothing else. When you went to the sweetstuff shop, you went to buy sweets, and that was all you could buy in that shop. To-day, one doesn't know where one is, or what shop is what; and I often wonder how the owners of some shops describe their business. Having renounced specialisation, they seem anxious to display versatility. You see a sign announcing a chemist's shop. You enter, and you find, first, a lending library; then a leather-goods counter; then a stationery counter; then a counter of silver knick-knacks. You find that the London chemist's activities are now as heterogeneous as those of a New York drugstore. Elsewhere you find provision-merchants selling sporting equipment; gramophone makers selling refrigerators; tobacconists selling cutlery; cutlers selling foreign stamps; greengrocers selling butter and eggs, and bookshops selling gramophone records. Very soon, I fancy, we shall not be able to speak of the grocer's shop or the confectioner's; we shall have to speak, as they do in villages, of The Shop. Not only in the great streets but in the minor streets of all parts of London one notes how many shops have ceased to be identified with the one kind of commodity proper to their business. One can understand a small concern embracing new lines touching its business. But these small concerns don't do that; they seem to look around for the most incongruous side-line. When you find shops mixing sewing-machines and Egyptian pottery; face-cream and pedigree pups; Gladstone bags and marmalade; you may be excused for thinking that commerce has fallen under the control of the Walrus, the Carpenter and the White Knight.

And you may be justified in wishing for the days of your youth, when shopping was perhaps more bothersome but less complicated by abortive efforts at simplifying it. In the dingy offices of the old days, men kept their letters in open trays on their desks, and when they wanted a particular letter they routed through each basket until they found it. Bothersome but certain. They kept their collars and shirts and studs in one drawer, so that the hunt was narrowed to one spot. In the kitchens the cooks had every utensil lying untidily about them. When you wanted your hoe you went to the garden-shed and routed for it. There was no neat little hoe-container to look for first--and find empty. A slow business, perhaps; almost as slow as the solving of one of Powys Mather's cross-words; but you knew where to look for what you wanted, and you knew that it wasn't disguised. To-day, all departments of life are so simplified that for almost every occasion one needs a code and an index. In the past, shopkeepers knew their own minds and minded their own business. They described themselves on their shop-fronts in terms of definition. The butcher was a "purveyor of meat." The greengrocer was a "pea and potato salesman." The man who sold hats was a hatter and it was useless to ask him for overcoats or skis. The man who sold milk was a "cow-keeper and dairyman." He might supply butter and cheese, which are of the dairy; he had no coffee or tinned peaches. The man who sold fowls and game was a "poulterer," with no interest in hair-dressing or confectionery. The stationer sold stationery, the fruiterer sold fruit and the florist sold flowers, and they left each other alone. None of them had a tobacco licence. To-day, as I say, few businesses remain faithful to the line of their origin, and their habit of encroaching on other lines may in time spread to the professions. Already actresses and baronets run millinery shops, and many an Army officer combines his military life with a business life on the boards of City companies. We may live to see ornaments of the Bar practising as M.D. as well as K.C., solicitors opening dental surgeries, professors of music running a sideline as Commissioners for Oaths.

It springs, I suppose, from the general expansion of life, the widening of interests, and the desire, which the physical bulk of London signifies, for More and Bigger. But the widening, I think, carries often the penalty of thinning. When you have too many things to look at it is not easy to derive much from any of them. And as between the large and the small, the small is often richer in content. I like all this space and variety and crashing colour and immensity, but there are times when I like a rest from it; times when I like to pause at a shop-window which displays one hat or one bottle of claret, one box of tea or one fountain-pen. Even at Christmas-time, when one looks for and allows a flourish of display, the windows seem to be overdone. Christmas may be the feast of plenty, but nobody wants too much of everything, and all in mammoth proportions. Profusion stupefies where economy stimulates. After looking at the Christmas shops of recent years, I find it restful to remember the Christmas displays of the little shops of the Diamond Jubilee year.

It is, I suppose, because one was young that one found them more alluring, more significant of festival, more charged with spirit than the lavish and gigantic exhibitions of these days. Or were they truly so? It is possible that they were, for each of them was a single voice giving out its little carol, and therefore more intimate in its message than the massed choirs of to-day. They were just little shops selling toys, "gifts," and other bright merchandise of the season, and they remained shops. They did not trespass into other fields and give us ballets, lectures, transformation-scenes and World's Fairs. The spirit of the season was present in each of those little shops. It was not driven into a corner by displays in its honour more concerned with the display than with the subject. When you had made your purchases in these shops, you were not given free rides to the South Pole, or free aeroplane trips, or presents from the mammoth Christmas Tree. The proprietors manifested the spirit of the season by presenting you with one coloured air-balloon. Therein I think they were right, since one trifling symbol is always more potent and expressive of an idea than twenty or thirty.

A London toyshop in those benighted days considered that it had only to be a shop which sold toys. It did not feel that Christmas was any occasion for gutting itself and becoming an Eskimo igloo or an Arizona ranch or an Ancient Briton's cave. The blessed word sophisticated (pronounced in the less elegant circles "fed-up") was not then the watchword of everybody over twelve. Our little minds were prepared to be amused by little things, and if a toyshop was frankly and sufficiently a toyshop, we made no complaint because it wasn't something else. We found quite enough interest in the small stock of goods; enough to keep us worried for some days in coming to a choice.

But maybe the children of this age are adjusted to Plethora and Colossus. Maybe the modern Christmas bazaar, with its two whole floors and basement of toys and games, and its half-dozen side-shows, its radio music and its three Father Christmases, does not bewilder the young as it bewilders me. Anyway, in rebuking myself for finding rapture in the backward view, I may console myself with the knowledge that when the present young are middle-aged, and are faced with still larger stores, they will be doing the same. They will be looking back just as wistfully at the quiet little Christmas stores they used to know--little six-storey affairs, with only three restaurants and two bands--and will be telling the spoiled youngsters how much more fun could be got out of those simplicities than the spoiled youngsters can get.

And the spoiled youngsters, reaching from the fireside for the televisor, and calling up the stores and asking the assistant to explain and show them on the screen the new models of party frocks, will pity their old aunts. Or, more likely, won't be listening.

WAR

The nineteenth century entered upon its final paroxysms with the coming of the war, and from 1914 to 1919 London was an anomalous creature going through paroxysms of its own in its approach to the new century. These were not immediately perceptible to common observation. It appeared to be going about its affairs in the normal way, only faintly perturbed by the horror just over the sea. But closer observation revealed undertones of strain and stress. It was not itself and it was not definitely anything else. Outwardly, it was a London of calm faces, of blue lamps, of women in uniform, and of deliberate geniality. A ruffled London denying to the world that it was ruffled. A London such as no Londoner, present or past, had seen or imagined, but which, when it came, was accepted as natural. As the capital of England and the English, it reflected the English attitude and feeling towards catastrophe, and whatever the failure on the part of the leaders may have been, this attitude and feeling lent as much credit to the common English as any victory of arms or diplomacy. The splendid feature of this time was the tone of the people of every rank, both those in uniform and those without; and in London it could be perceived in the whole. A stranger, noting the prosperity of the theatres, music-halls, restaurants and hotels, might have been excused for thinking that London could never have been so bright. But London was not bright. It was *being* bright; keeping up its spirits and the spirits of the men on leave; and the effect was as strained as when a once-brilliant actor is being brilliant. Everything of the grim and horrid was hidden. The pestilence was treated as new material for jests and japes. People tacitly agreed to accept the brimstone from the sky as if it were rain; and after the first six months one had the feeling, in London at any rate, that war was a constant state and that we had always lived with it.

Looking at the papers of the period gives one little idea of the purgatory through which Europe was passing, and the repercussion of it all upon London. The "lead" stories, streamed across three columns, are of "Great British Advance" or "Peace Overtures," and the leading article tackles some problem of the war as affecting civilians, or rates Whitehall for its management of affairs in France and elsewhere. But the bulk of the paper--all papers then were reduced in size--is much what it is to-day. That is--gossip; woman's column; notices of new plays, new books, new concerts; sport; crime; finance; accidents, and all the minutiæ of the everyday round. Where a story impinges upon the war, it is so treated as to suggest that there is nothing the Londoner so much enjoys as war. The general note was: "This is the Great War. Have a good time, everybody!"

This was the attitude not only of the popular press, but of popular entertainment and of social intercourse. Those four years bore, I think, more colloquial stories, printable and unprintable, than any previous twenty.

Every new development of the situation brought its own crop of anecdote. There were stories about medical examinations--hundreds of these. Stories about the bantam regiments; about women bus-conductors, about the W.A.A.C. and the W.R.N.S. Stories about ration-cards, and about meatless days, and air raids; about Pink Forms and Blue Forms, and even about wounded soldiers. No aspect was free from Rabelaisian treatment by the great unknown who create these masterpieces of the short story. In the little magazines produced by the men at the front something of the same spirit prevailed. All that war had meant to past generations, all its epic colour and grandeur which the poets and artists had shed upon it, were, by the soldiers of this war, deliberately guyed. Any popular songs which celebrated the splendour of the forces, or any people or group of people who tried to make a sentimental fuss of the fighting men, were rewarded by a riposte of derision. And derision was their response to those hysterical girls who sent white feathers to middle-aged actors and others who were not in uniform. The songs appreciated by them were songs with a gibe in them--"Fred Karno's Army," "Send My Mother," "Take Me Back to Blighty," "Oh, It's A Lovely War." Those strange and tragic years afforded many new sidelights on human nature, but nothing, I think, was stranger than this human and heroic passion for turning misery into farce, and sacrifice into a joke.

One of these minor sidelights was the extraordinary appetite that arose in people of all kinds for humble and hitherto despised foods which happened to be scarce. In ordinary life most people can live comfortably without potatoes. Many do. Some don't care for them, and others rule them out as fattening. But on the first hint of a shortage of potatoes everybody discovered a yearning for potatoes, and any shop which was serving potatoes drew a queue not only of poor people, to whom the potato was a useful adjunct of meals, but of the well-to-do. Numbers of people would see a queue outside a provision shop, and would automatically join it, without troubling to inquire whether it was offering turnips, biscuits or tripe. Some who had gone through life with no taste for figs, would suddenly find that figs were essential to comfort, and would go to great trouble and loss of time to extract an illicit box of figs from a compliant grocer. I knew a man who never ate jam, and who had no children, for whom, I suppose, jam is mainly produced. But when jam was rationed, this man, otherwise doing his duty as a reliable citizen, hearing that jam could be had at a North London shop without inquiries, made the journey from Surrey to North London and returned in triumph with one pot of jam. This exploit became his favourite and most tiresome anecdote.

Little could then be forecast about the attitudes and responses of the average man. He afforded a succession of surprises; notably when one remembered the popular attitude to the Boer War. I had no close observation of the effect of this upon London and London life. I was at school at the time, and caught only echoes of it from illustrated papers and popular songs. But I do know from hearsay that London went hysterical over this small adventure of crushing a group of farmers who had no regular army. It was seen as a mighty conflict in which the soul of England was the stake. Every victory of the trained soldiers over the burghers was regarded as an occasion for jubilee rejoicings and as one more proof that England was master of the world and mistress of the seas. This may have been because England had not, for nearly a century, been engaged in a real war, and took this miniature affair as an example of a Great War, with Kruger as Napoleon. Anyway, it was the last outburst of jingoism of which we have been guilty, for when the Great War did come, and brought disaster to almost every home, and attack upon our coasts and towns, there was neither moaning nor rejoicing. None of the events of those four years produced a "Relief of Ladysmith" excitement or a "Relief of Mafeking" debauchery. Gains and losses were accepted as facts. Nobody hung out flags because of gains, or talked of what Old England could do. Nobody went sick because of losses. No songs were written about the battle of the Somme of the kind that were written about Spion Kop and Graspan. The spirit of London and of the nation remained imperturbable; the Boer War had taught a lesson.

All the popular songs of the 1899 affair that I heard at school were, as I say, of a distinctly jingo kind; those that were not were of the "sob" kind. There were songs about British Pluck and about Going to Fight the Foe. Men who were boys when I was a boy may remember some of them. "Break the News to Mother," "Bravo, the

Dublin Fusiliers," "Bugler Dunne," "Good-bye, my Bluebell," and that neuralgic example of what a great writer and a distinguished composer can do in their off-moments--"The Absent-Minded Beggar." Those songs were the last wag of the old tail. Nothing of their note was to be heard in the popular songs made during 1914-1918. In the fourteen years between the two wars the English had acquired a new dignity and a wider outlook. Something of the spirit foreshadowed in Sir William Watson's Coronation Ode of 1902 had visited them. They knew that this was a testing time, and no time for heroics; and apart from that, they were a generation which had no use for the pearly lorgnette of sentiment. They wanted to look at life straight. Hence the note of all the songs was a mocking of the earlier note. The men knew no great battles. They took part in a "show" at Festubert, or a "show" at Paschendaele, or a "show" at Jutland. They gave pet names to the enemy--Fritz and Jerry. They gave pet names to his weapons. They wrote parodies on songs about courage and about the splendour of war.

This spirit was reflected to London and appeared, as I say, in the attitude of the people and in all references to the war. A small section of the press, and an occasional fugitive song, tried to keep up the old stuff by speaking of every British soldier as a hero, and every German as a coward, but in time even this section was laughed out of it by the soldiers themselves. During those years London was a city in the war-zone which went on with its business and at the same time made itself a playground for men of the forces on leave. It had no flags for them; no cheers; but it had what was more appreciated--a spirit of fellowship and lots of entertainment. It was an ungainly London to which we introduced them, but at that time appearances didn't count. It was out of joint physically, and in a state of flux spiritually; yet, with its natural flexibility, it managed still to be London. Hotels had become Government offices, and Government offices had become dormitories. Parks and squares had become market-gardens, and superannuated actors came forward to make the male choruses of musical shows. Disused shops and houses had become recruiting centres, and every kind of works a munition factory. Skilled labour was being rewarded as it had never before been rewarded--or since; and the decorators of life, the gilt of civilisation, who had formerly been its pets, had become ten a penny. Buildings which had been in course of erection at the outbreak remained for four years like Jezreel's Towers, showing their bare bones and eyeless sockets to the London sky; while on the vacant sites of Aldwych and Bloomsbury, Y.M.C.A. huts and soldiers' recreation-rooms were run up overnight. Indeed, wherever there was a vacant site, there were huts. Along the main roads on the outskirts, little towns of hutments were built in a week or so for munition workers; but for any other kind of building there was no time, money, or labour.

As the war dragged on the city became more and more dingy. Renovation and repainting had to be held over, and only urgently necessary road-work was done.

But though its face was unkempt and grey, it maintained a level mood of cheerfulness. The grief that visited so many homes kept itself hidden for the sake of others and for the preservation of the general strength, and there was a top current of geniality and a new affability. Under the stress of the times, English reserve disappeared. Men developed a habit of talking fraternally with strangers, regardless of what schools the fellows went to. In 1917 a constant cause of this fraternising was a day of rain. That kind of day, before and since, usually produced peevish faces; in those years it was an occasion for smiles. Men said to each other: "This is good. They can't come in this." "They," of course, was that new peril from the sky which resembled no peril through which the people of London had hitherto passed. When it came, it was accepted, by the majority, with that phlegm which so amuses the Latin.

London knew many perils during this period, but the one peril common to Londoners of every sort was this air peril. It was this, perhaps, above the general fact of war and suffering, which brought them together and created and maintained that mood of cheerfulness. Many prophets had visualised a war in which "flying-machines" had appeared over London and bombed it, and had pictured the panic and the flight of the people. What would be the reaction of a city to a constant daily and nightly bombardment from the air, nobody at present can tell; it probably would be as prophesied--evacuation and surrender. But so far as the few and intermittent raids of the last war went, the prophets were wrong. The first raids aroused curiosity more than any other emotion, and even the more regular visits, during the September of 1917, only slightly disturbed the surface of London's routine. Business proceeded normally. Restaurants and entertainments continued their service. People in the streets were ordered by the police to Take Cover, and were marshalled into the Tube stations. Trains halted where they happened to be on the warning of the maroons, and householders took their families to the cellar and played cards until the Boy Scouts' bugles announced the All Clear. Air-raid parties between neighbours were a feature of that year.

Often during dinner in a restaurant one would hear the boom of the maroons, and the company would look about and say "They're Over." At a particularly fierce crash, the remark would be: "Pretty close, that one." That was all. Dinner went on, and the orchestra went on, and from the atmosphere of the room and the demeanour of the people and the staff the year might have been any peace year. One of the oddest experiences in an odd London, but one accepted then as part of normal life, was to be sitting in the Aldwych Theatre, during Sir Thomas Beecham's opera season, listening to "The Magic Flute" or "The Marriage of Figaro," while the barrage crashed and rumbled overhead. This I knew three or four times, and on each occasion not more than a dozen people left the theatre. In music-halls, the situation was treated by the comedians with gags--feeble, perhaps, but effective in their moment. "Hush--I forbid the bangs"; or "I don't like you in green. Run and put on your maroon frock."

The entertainers, I think, more than anybody, helped to nourish the cheerful spirit of the town. The spirit was there to begin with, of course, but they gave it tone. Sir Thomas Beecham notably deserves credit for preserving to us a little oasis of grace and light in a time when all else was darkness and violence. Those opera seasons of his maintained the balance of many a man who might otherwise have fallen to nervous bitterness and melancholia; and for the larger public there were vaudeville and gay musical shows, which performed a similar service. Mr. St. John Ervine, in his volume of this series dealing with the Theatre, speaks with distaste of the war-time productions. To some extent I agree with him. Their promoters set out ostensibly to cater for a standardised person whom they called "Tommy," without any first-hand knowledge of "Tommy's" taste and intelligence. They seemed to assume that the private soldier of this war was identical with the private soldier of 1881. Still, there were a few sensible productions which did not underrate the intelligence of the average man. I did not see them, not being a theatre man, but I heard about them; and from my own observation I know how thickly each audience of Beecham opera was sprinkled with uniform.

The street scene of this time had somewhat the nature of the first-act crowd in the town-square of a light opera. Soldiers and sailors were as frequent as civilians, and costumes and uniforms were of all kinds. Besides the British uniforms, there were Canadian, Australian and American uniforms; and here and there a French, Belgian, Italian or Serbian uniform. There were special constables and ambulance men. There were the khaki women of the W.A.A.C., the blue women of the W.R.N.S. and the women of the Red Cross. There were Y.M.C.A. uniforms and Church Army uniforms. There were Boy Scouts and Girl Guides. There were the short-skirted women bus-conductors and women taxi-drivers, the women guards and porters of the Underground, and the brown-frocked girl-messengers of the Government offices. A few civilians, having no uniforms or medals or ribbons, but feeling a need of decoration of some kind, went about with buttons in their coats, inscribed "Intern Them All." In some of the minor departments of life a new note was perceptible--a little garnish of Latin customs. Young soldiers on leave, who had hitherto been roast-beef men, brought home a taste for the dishes of France or Eastern Europe. With the entrance of large numbers of refugees from Belgium and the invaded French areas, came many new restaurants which filled the gap left by those German restaurants which had closed themselves at the outbreak of war or had been smashed by the mob in the riots following the sinking of the *Lusitania*. (One episode which reflected no credit on the London scene or the deportment of Londoners during those four years.) Belgian patisseries and the French café-bar, complete with zinc counter, arrived, and have remained a constant feature of the central streets. Paris journals and the Caporal cigarette were on sale everywhere. French revues were brought to the theatres. Soho had a boom period. America introduced us to its cafeterias and snack-bars, and to the ball game. Athens opened a couple of restaurants, and the provision shops dressed their windows with exotic foods which we found pleasant after butcher's offal and mangel-wurzel and stewed goat. Insularity disappeared, and for that period London was truly cosmopolitan.

Certain days of this long winter stand out as expressive of the whole drama. There was that August Bank Holiday of 1914, when the atmosphere was so charged with portent that the most insensitive were aware of it, and Hampstead Heath went through its motions with a preoccupied air. There was that day when the first news of the Jutland battle gave us the impression that the Navy had been annihilated. There was the first air-raid by Zeppelins, when one of them was brought down at Potters Bar, and crowds on the Embankment saw the flaming mass falling through the air, and tried to cheer, and somehow couldn't. There was the day when the Gothas came at noon. There was another noon when London streets were filled with blank faces and wondering eyes; when a pang greater than that caused by any air-raid seemed to go through the city. It was the noon when the evening-paper bills said: "Kitchener Drowned." The public had invested that name with a sort of ju-ju magic, and for the first hour the news was received as a sign that England was undone.

And finally there was that morning of November 1918 when, at a signal from the maroons, offices and houses were emptied, and the streets were filled, and faces turned towards St. James Park and the Green Park. Nobody who witnessed that descent on the park can forget it. The signal was expected at eleven o'clock. At half-past ten the park held only a handful of people. By three minutes past eleven, the Mall was a dense mass of people marching twenty or more abreast, and from every gate thousands more poured in to join it. One instinct seized all who were in central London at that hour-- Buckingham Palace; and to the Palace they marched, laughing, cheering, singing, weeping, and the King and Queen came out to the balcony to greet them. The moment was aptly caught by Siegfried Sassoon in his poem--"Everyone suddenly burst out singing." It was not, as I have said, the cheap ballyhoo of Mafeking Night. There was excitement, and, to some extent, hysteria; but it had a more serious basis than the other affair. It was no celebration of victory and the boys of the bull-dog breed. It was a gasp of relief as at the sudden cessation of a pain which all peoples had been suffering. Even the rackety scenes that occurred at night in some parts of town arose rather from sobbing thankfulness than from jubilation; and one felt that the people who were building bonfires in Trafalgar Square, and those who were hanging over the sides of buses, and those who were getting tight in bars, were all the time on the verge of tears.

But the feature of those years of London's story which remains persistently in the memory is the nights. One never could take them for granted as one took the other conditions of war. As each new and sharp change in our habits and surroundings arrived, it took London but a day or two to adjust itself to them. An innovation of Monday was by Saturday a custom. But the new lighting of London was a recurring phenomenon. Each evening was a mild shock. London by day wore an odd face, but it was still London. This night-London seemed a changeling. One wandered about it, knowing that one was in London, but unable to locate its features and spirit. All outdoor lamps were painted blue, and all shop and house lights thickly screened. All public-houses were shut at half-past nine, and almost every shop. Theatres, music-halls and a few restaurants only were open after ten. Entertainment and distraction of other sorts were held behind closed doors.

Stevenson should have seen this new London. He could have placed in it a New Arabian Night which would have topped all the others in the extravagant and bizarre. Side by side with sorrow and apprehension went curious hushed orgies. Many of the things that happened at that time in this blinded city will never be known; one can only guess at them from the happenings that one did hear about or witness. As no drinks were publicly to be got after half-past nine, men created speak-easies for themselves. I have heard of men who held bottle-parties in the little boxes of lavatory attendants, or took their bottles and sat round the camp-fire with nightwatchmen at "road-up" points. Coffee-stalls were well patronised; chiefly for their cups and lemonade glasses. Among a certain small section air-raid nights afforded occasions for pyjama parties. Their attitude seemed to be; To-morrow We Die. Their feeling about dying was stoical; they held roof entertainments during the raids; and they seemed to see the war as a licence for doing things they formerly would have liked to do but had not done; and the blue-lit London of this period was their ally. It was also an ally for wild people of another order, but I believe the four years showed no increase of street crime and assault. Those eclipsed streets, coming so suddenly after the new brilliance of public and shop lighting to which we had become accustomed, and thus confusing us, gave notable opportunity to the law's enemies. But it was not taken. Not until well after the war did the hold-up men operate on any large scale, and then they chose not the night hours and dim-lit squares but broad daylight and crowded highways. I have heard this absence of crime lightly ascribed to the fact that all the "boys" were serving with the So-and-so's--various regiments to which the speaker did not belong--in the capacity of quartermasters. However it was, those benighted streets were as safe in all parts of town as when fully lit.

One groped about them, catching sometimes the horns of elfland and sometimes the whispers of nightmare, and one groped in peace, meeting no hazard save that from above. One had the feeling that London had been embalmed and bestowed in a mummy-case.

The outline was there and a representation of the features, but it was a case only, and the thing itself was hidden. Brilliant searchlights probed and wiped the sky; we of the streets lived in a blue mist, and seemed to breathe blue mist. A few years earlier the possibility of making such a great city as London invisible from above would have been dismissed. But between 1914 and 1918 many former "impossibilities" became facts, and one of them was this night-cloaking of London. Many of those phosphorescent nights I spent rambling about a London I knew so well, and discovering, under the new lighting, strange shapes on familiar streets, strange atmospheres in commonplace corners, strange aspects of Oxford Street and Victoria Street which I had never before noted. Cloak though it was, it served also to reveal, and in this it was more effective than all your flood-lighting. Reticence always carries more truthful pointers to angles and recesses of character than confession, and in those years one came to "know" London better than before, as one may suddenly know a new friend when he stops talking and sits for an hour by the fire in twilight and silence. It was, as I say, a London one never got used to, and perhaps because of that it came closer and helped us to know it by presenting a new phase every night. When, at the end of 1918, the blinds were raised and the paint removed from the street lamps, the effect, though welcome after the long dusk, was so garish that it worried the eyes and disturbed the mind. Once again we were *seeing* London by night, and it went one remove back from the time when we had been feeling it.

Oddly enough, those years showed little change in the Londoner's outlook and temper. The change was in process of making, and the period was a spasm of labour between the old and the new. It was the agony of Springtime and rebirth. Not until the twenties did we see the full effect of the times in new attitudes, new demands, new forms of entertainment, new modes of speech, new crime, and a new and more violent loosening, especially among the young, of all old restraints. The cry on all sides was for A Good Time. The social type of the pre-war years went into hiding, and left the new type to carry on one long Whoopee.

It seemed that the thunder of the guns and of anti-aircraft defence had so long tormented people's ears as to bring them to a state in which they could not live without it. More noise, they craved, more noise. And the theatres and the restaurants and the dance-halls and the electric-drills and the motor-bikes and the talkies supplied it. The amusements of the twenties must go on record, I think, as the apotheosis of noise. Noise was their essence, their structure, their whole being; when drum and saxophone and cymbals ceased to have effect upon the drugged ear, it was re-galvanised by semi-human voices reproducing the bayings of the jungle. People of every sort loved it; it was a necessary adjunct to their idea of a Good Time. Anything serene was dull; anything *piano* was unheard, and was none the sweeter for that. Everything must be *prestissimo* and *fortissimo*. Fashionable restaurants and night-clubs were temples of the god of Din, to whom the best people paid homage.

The female voice became a screech, and physical manners based themselves on the catherine-wheel.

The outstanding mania of a maniac period was the party-mania. Parties were always a natural part of the life of those whose time is their own, but in former days they were kept in their place. In the twenties they became the whole of social life. A party every night, given or attended, was not sufficient; young people entered into competition on the number of parties they could "look in at" in a given night. So eager did they become in this pursuit that they ceased to pay attention to the elementary matter of invitations; they introduced to London one more American touch. They showed us that good manners were made only for the stodgy, and that for ardent spirits rules of conduct must give way. They introduced us to gate-crashing. Happily, it and they lasted but a short time. What codes of decency or paternal authority could not accomplish was accomplished by the economic slump. Easy money vanished, and under apprehensions of disaster the party mania vanished, and the Bright Young Things and their capers.

London life of that period will afford rather a puzzle to future social historians. It will not, as I have said, yield much in the way of sharp-flavoured character, but it will yield an odd array of follies, against which those of the Regency or the D'Orsay period seem almost staid. And it might yield as much scandal as the Restoration period. But it will be lifeless stuff, empty ho-de-ho noise with no mind or temperament to crystallise it. Fashion is always self-conscious about itself and its doings, but the nineteen-twenties, I think, excelled all other ages in this adolescent trait. Through all its embarrassing behaviour it was crying "Look at me!", and when people looked and were not amused it was undismayed. But it has learned now that life is not a bowl of cherries or a scat-song. It has learned that life is real and earnest. Its more able members have gone into business; others have realised the fatuity of those years and have settled down and said Good-bye to all that hullabaloo. The present younger set is altogether different. It is more responsible in its attitude and more sensible in its demeanour. It has gentler faces, gentler manners, and is as naturally bright as the others tried to be.

Those manifestations of tarantism, pointless as they appear, afford fruitful material for that modern "Vanity Fair" which every modern novelist thinks about and always shies from writing. But the real significance of that saturnalia of the twenties is that it was our welcome to the new century.

ENTERTAINMENT

The fading of the music-hall from the London scene, which I regretted earlier, has been in process for some years. Vaudeville is still not wholly gone, but it is no longer a natural part of the furniture of the people's recreation. It began to suffer a change with the American invasion of 1909 and the substitution of flaring and blaring revues for the native man-to-man appeal. It suffered a distinct set-back when, a little later, the movies made their crashing assault upon the threepences and sixpences of the poorer people. And when the twentieth century began in 1920, it seemed to be doomed. It may come back to us, but it can never come back in its old style and spirit. The life and character and scene which it represented are gone. The types, both high and low, which it ridiculed are gone. Red noses and eccentric costume are no longer in favour. Humour, for the time being, has had to give way to wit.

The music-hall which I knew in the nineteen-noughts could not have stayed long with us, since it was, like many other London features which have only lately gone, a hang-over from the nineteenth century. It was the comic spirit of an age, and when that age passed it, too, had to pass. It had to give way to a new and younger kind of entertainment--lighter, thinner, more polished, more conscious of itself. The concert form of entertainment, centring round a dress-suit and a piano, or a dance-band and a drilled chorus. Cabaret is the expression of the present age, and it serves it as aptly as music-hall served the past age. Music-hall was but one of many hang-overs. Comic journalism also remained for some time definitely of the past century, and lingered on in the form of *Pick-me-up, Judy, Ally Sloper, Scraps, Moonshine, Sketchy Bits, Photo Bits.* The spirit of these journals was the spirit of the old halls, and that there is still a public reverting to that spirit is shown by the success of the English *Razzle* and the American *Ballyhoo,* which are sort of nephews of those journals.

The music-hall was never, like current entertainment, an acidulous critic of life. It had no Voltaire. It was instead a hearty acceptance of life, and its presiding lord was Falstaff. Its funniest jokes centred on the woes of poverty, and its audience, mainly poor people, accepted them with relish. It gave neither sneer nor civil leer. It laughed at its audience, and its audience laughed back. Of taste it knew nothing, but while some of its coarsenesses would affront modern ears, it is equally true that some of the smirking innuendoes of modern cabaret songs, longing to be completely French yet not quite daring, would affront those who laughed at the old music-hall. It sang and told, without finesse, of tripe, kippers, mothers-in-law, lodgers and adultery, garters and lingerie. It put no burnished gleam or rose-pink twilight of art on these things. It did not dress them in evening clothes. It presented them in their everyday earthiness and left it at that. The only comedy it knew was the elemental comedy of disaster. The only drama it knew concerned A Woman's Honour. But it was rich mixture, dug direct from English soil. To-day there is little soil from which to dig it. Classes no longer live in their own tight compartments, and, as I said earlier, individual and typical oddity have been obliterated. Without them, music-hall of the kind we middle-aged people knew cannot live. It may survive, but only, I think, as the fair and the circus survive, or Punch and Judy.

What chiefly comes to mind when thinking of music-hall is its songs. I don't know what was in the air at that time, from 1897 to 1909, but all the songs I remember, especially the wildly comic songs, had in their melodies a pathos that beat unbearably on the heart. They were songs intended to rouse Homeric laughter, or to prod you with memories of rude and raffish nights in the West End; and all they did was to play upon the nerves with a Verlaine tristesse. The airs of those songs, when I recall them, evoke for me the sadness of London streets in October twilights; crying children; the throb of London life coming muted over intervening roofs. Many a time, when wandering through rainy suburban byways, I have had my blood chilled almost to tears by a distant organ playing the latest comic song. Time may have done something to one's memory of them, as Time has done something to the little dance-airs which one hears on musical-boxes of a hundred years ago; jolly little airs when they were made, though for us full of pathos. But think of the air of "She was a Dear Little Dicky Bird," of "A Fair Old Rickety-Rackety Crew," of "Our Lodger's

Such a Nice Young Man," of "All Round the Houses," and of "It's a Different Girl Again." It isn't entirely due to Time that one hears the shyly-poignant note of grief. The note is there as clearly as it is in the airs of Tschaikowsky. It is the note of the London streets, and if you seek a true musical expression of London you are nearer to it in these rough comic songs than in such considered works as Elgar's "Cockaigne" overture or Vaughan Williams' "London" Symphony.

For music-hall songs of those days were made by the people for the people. They were not made, as popular songs are made to-day, by sleek young men living in Piccadilly flats and drawing, by various "rights," two and three thousand pounds from a song which has a run of four months. A few guineas was the general reward then, though the composers had that other reward desired by the poet who cared not who made the nation's laws so that he might make its songs. Their songs did not have a run of four months: they had a run of some years, long enough to sink into the public memory and become the heritage and expression of an age. That they did sink in is proved by their immense popularity when the B.B.C. revives them and sends them across the air. In the library of my ears I hold an anthology of them. The earliest item is one sung by Gus Elen, concerning the view that might be had from his London garden "if it wasn't for the houses in between"; and by succeeding items I can date the stages of my life more clearly than by the years of the calendar.

One reason why they had a long life and sank into the public mind was that there were not then the mechanical means that exist to-day for thrusting them upon the entire British public in one week. There was only the street-organ to carry them to those who did not frequent music-halls, and even the organs took some time to cover their itinerary. Also, people did not then demand constant change; they were willing to hear a comedian sing again the songs he sang last year or the year before; even to demand them. "Back numbers," so far from being scorned, were petted, and some comedians, who themselves were sick of their songs, were often thwarted in their efforts to introduce new songs. No matter what new things Chirgwin tried to present; the audience would give them a patient hearing, and then would come the plaintive cry--"Blind Boy, George; Blind Boy!" To-day, the case is reversed; a singer may not sing in Spring the songs he was singing the previous Autumn. Mechanical devices transport them to millions of ears soon after their introduction, and his potential audience is soon used up. Thus the public has none of that long-continued acquaintance with songs, as part of an age's voice, which enabled people of the past to link them with their little private epochs. A comedian then could launch his new song in London, and take it on tour, and wherever he went it would be new. It never got ahead of him. By the time he got back to London he could offer it again to London audiences, and they would welcome it, and cherish it for him. There is a certain song of the past by which I date all the happenings of a certain two years. I cannot name those two years; I only know that during that period the nerves of the London streets were tingling with a plaintive melody which so worked itself into the woof of London and into all my occasions that whenever I recall a few bars of it I recall also all my affairs and all the London scene of that period. I know it as the "Hiawatha" period.

The hold which the music-hall had on the people was as firm as the present hold of the movies, and perhaps more deeply founded. In London to-day, at the moment of writing, there are five music-halls operating as music-halls, and in the near suburbs scarcely half-a-dozen more. Up to 1912, as I have said, there were in central London and the near suburbs over forty. The London halls were the Alhambra, Palace, Empire, Hippodrome, Coliseum, Palladium, Canterbury, Pavilion, Middlesex, Metropolitan, Oxford, Holborn, Tivoli, and Victoria Palace. The principal suburban halls were the South London, the Empress, the Duchess, the New Bedford, the London, the Euston, the Cambridge, Collins', and the Alexandra.

Almost every suburb had its hall, and for the younger working-people it was a sort of social centre in a way the movie-palace cannot be. In a music-hall the people were together, often packed tightly together; and they could see each other and hear each other. But in the movie-palace they gather in the dark, and, however full the place may be, there is no feeling of being together. Despite the popularity of the "theme-song," you never hear them join in the choruses. They are units or couples, enclosed in separate bowls of darkness, and though this may be appreciated by sentimental couples it goes oddly against the spirit of this age, which is all towards communal amusement, communal feeding and communal labour. In the past people were individuals who liked, now and then, to gather at a music-hall and be one of a great mass. To-day, in our general life, we are but one of a mass, and can only recover our individuality by going to the movies and enclosing ourselves in the opaque bit of gloom allotted to us. Perhaps that, among other things, is why the movies are so successful. Not only do they give the poor what the poor of this age love to see--not the comic pictures of themselves which amused their fathers, but pictures of gilded palaces, "luxury" hotels, platinum bathrooms and enamel blondes, steel-true and blade-straight heroes, million-dollar night-clubs and a world where money is as common as dust in the parlour. Not only do they give the poor these Arabian pipe-dreams; they provide also an anodyne to the mass-instincts of these times. The young working-people consciously like them for the Arabian Night stuff, and would rather go alone to see a bad movie than go with two or three others to see a good music-hall. But it may be that unconsciously they like the movies and their surroundings for the opportunity they give for withdrawal into themselves and escape from crowd action and crowd thought.

The rapid growth in popularity of this form of entertainment is a sign of the modern speed of things. In these days one may present a novelty to the public, win their approval of it, load them with it and sicken them of it, and retire with a fortune--all in the time it formerly took to introduce a novelty. I do not know how long the music-hall took, from its early beginnings, to fix a hold on the English public, but I am willing to bet that it was twenty times as long as it took the movies. In 1908 the movies were practically unknown to intelligent people. They were then shyly showing themselves (strange to reflect that the movies *were* once shy) in parish halls and in little fit-up places in side streets of the poorer quarters, and were mainly patronised by children--as they still are, if we stretch the term "children." At first the performers were anonymous; nobody thought that the public could possibly care about the lay figures who were going through those banal motions. A little later they were given nick-names of the crude schoolboy sort--"Fatty," "Skinny," etc. There came a time when a man mentioned to me with surprise that his children, who were receiving a serious education, were infatuated with this idiotic entertainment, and, rising to a note of astonishment, said that the children actually knew the names of the people who were photographed doing those silly things. That man has passed away. Had he lived through the movie age he would have been gradually accustomed to finding these photographed people receiving the homage of the great, plus an income of two thousand pounds a week. Had I been able to tell him, at the time he was talking to me, that it would come to that, he would have been rude--and with justice. Nevertheless, it has come, and stranger things yet will come.

By 1915 the movies were everywhere and were everybody's entertainment. In eight years they had conquered London and England. By 1920 the intellectuals were taking them up, examining them, discussing them, ranking them; and Charles Chaplin, whose comedy was discovered and whose fortune was made by poor children, became an "artist," and serious essays were written upon his technique. They are now as much a part of everybody's life as the daily paper. You may be, like myself, one who does not care for them and does not go to see them, but you can no more escape them and their influence than you can escape the influence of the *Daily* ---- which you never read. They have reached the point now where they can erect their palaces in such once-august spots as Curzon Street and Park Lane; and where a film "first-night" produces as brilliant an assembly as a reception at a great embassy.

They are, as I say, everybody's entertainment, but they could not have been that without the help of the poorer people. It was the threepences and sixpences of the side-street public of the past which built the palaces in the West End, and it needs a philosopher, possibly of the Viennese school, to tell us why. Given the points I have mentioned, of the Arabian Nights and the escape from crowd-contact, one would think the patrons would leave these places in a mood if not of delight at least of refreshment. But they don't. If you are old enough to remember the London and suburban music-halls, you will be able to recall the spectacle of the crowd when it came out. It came out, or poured out, bubbling. It came out humming choruses. It came out with bright eyes. At the worst, it came out cheerful. Watch the people coming from a movie-palace. They come out frowning. They come out without speaking. They come out as though there were nothing in life worth living for. They have had for their sixpence or shilling much more than the music-hall people of the gallery ever had--more in upholstery, more in imitation marble, more in regimental attendants, more in general comfort, and any one picture they have seen cost far more than the whole week's bill of a music-hall. The people of the old music-hall gallery came out as though Uncle John in Australia had left them a fortune. The movie audience comes out as though it has just left the sick-room of a poor relation.

The theatre, happily, is still a part of the London scene, though it is to-day more a function than an integral part of the life of the people. Despite the frequent building of new theatres, London is still, under the movie-conquest, below the pre-war period of this century in its number of theatres, and the suburbs are hopelessly outpointed. In 1912 central London had thirty-four regular theatres, not counting music-halls which occasionally lent themselves as theatres. Other parts of the town supported twenty-three more. To-day it is much below those numbers. The suburbs have lately broken out into experimental "little" theatres, but the majority of the old houses have disappeared, and only four remain in action. When I was a youth you could see a play with a "West End Company" at the Coronet, Notting Hill; the Marlborough, Holloway Road; the

Kennington; and the Borough, Stratford. You could also see plays at the Camden, Camden Town; the Dalston; the Surrey, Blackfriars; the Metropole, Camberwell, where I saw my first pantomime; the Elephant and Castle; the Crown, Peckham, and the Britannia, Hoxton. And there were the West London, off Edgware Road; the Crouch End Opera House; the Grand, at Woolwich; Terriss', at Deptford; the Grand, at Islington, and the Pavilion, at Mile End. But of course the young person, reading this, will say "Who wants to sit on a hard bench and see a play with only three changes of scene, when she can see two movie plays and a lot of news reels in comfort?" Given the young person's outlook, I think the young person has it. The theatres afford her no answer. The movies do. They have set themselves to be a part of her life, and they make it their business to serve her. The theatres go on expressing themselves. The movies go on impressing the young person. The contest recalls Spurgeon's advice to the candidate for ordination. He told the candidate to come to him and deliver a trial sermon, treating him as a congregation. The candidate delivered his trial sermon. Spurgeon's verdict was--"A good sermon. Remarkably good for one of your years. But quite useless. In that sermon you were engaged in expressing yourself. Your job, as a preacher, is to get something *into me*."

Spurgeon's name leads to another feature of London life which has suffered some decay; a feature which, though not properly to be called entertainment, was often so regarded. The vogue of the Great Preacher. As a boy I was often taken about to this form of instructional pastime, but as I was thinking all the time of that unfinished chapter of Talbot Baines Reed, I have no clear recollection of whom or what I heard. People went then to hear Great Preachers as to-day they go to the Albert Hall to hear great singers and musicians; and went with fervid interest. The last pulpit orator I can recall who could draw the London crowd with his oratorical fire is one who is no longer in London--R. J. Campbell. Before him they could be counted thickly. Spurgeon himself, Dr. Parker, F. B. Meyer, Bernard Vaughan, Hugh Price Hughes, and others whose names I once knew but cannot now recall. But I remember clearly how they were discussed and weighed and compared, and how Aunts would come with news of a wonderful preacher heard at some outlying church, in the manner of an impresario reporting to the opera-directors on a new Wotan. Parties would be made up to visit this discovery, and on return they would sit about criticising his matter, his delivery, his gestures, and how far he surpassed or fell short of their particular standards of unction and oratory.

The modern lack of stirring preachers is due, I suppose, to natural law. As a constant patronage of painting produces great painters, and a keen demand for opera produces great singers, so churches regularly filled with congregations spiritually awake, produce great preachers. When there is no public interest in painting there are no great painters, and half-empty churches and a tepid interest in the Church's life mean indifferent preaching. That was the situation up to the last few years, but lately there have been signs of change. We are beginning to hear of churches which are regularly filled, and of a widespread interest in the Sunday broadcast services, though the preaching I have heard is rather of the correct and arid order, wanting fire. From all sides we are learning of a religious revival, particularly among the young. Campaigns of all sorts are in progress, and all sorts of new bodies are gathering adherents. There is talk in newspapers about this new interest, this search of the young for Something in a reeling world, and many papers have taken to reporting religious activities. But religious revivals are not necessarily synonymous with spiritual revivals, and it is only from spiritual passion that great preaching is born. We have, I believe, as many stirring preachers among us to-day as the latter part of last century had. We shall hear them only when we indicate that we want to hear them; when the religious revival becomes a *spiritual* revival and our preachers are fertilised by the chemistry of their congregations' vision.

It may come, and it may come, paradoxically, from the change in the conduct of Sunday and in the public attitude towards it. The puritanical Sunday had little to do with things of the spirit. It was concerned with material things; with forms and ceremonies and groanings and other distractions from that quietude in which alone the spirit can grow. The modern Sunday has changed all that. Religious forms themselves have been simplified, and religion has not insisted that everybody shall walk in gloom, whether they accept the Thirty-nine Articles or not. A comparison of the London Sundays of to-day with Sundays so historically recent as those of the Diamond Jubilee year affords one of the most striking of all changes in the London picture. The London Sunday is still not what it might be, as the worker's day of freedom. It is still far from that goal of Satanism which certain minds express by the awful word "Continental." We are all familiar with a sentence which appears so regularly in the press on Monday mornings that I think all newspaper offices must keep it in stereo: "Nobody wishes to see the Continental Sunday introduced into England." Every time I see that sentence I wonder how many Continental Sundays the speakers have seen, and what degree of black iniquity is displayed by going respectably and quietly to fairs, circuses, theatres and operas on the one day of the week when the mass of the people have control of their own bodies and activities.

Dickens' pamphlet, "Sunday Under Three Heads," which gave sad pictures of the London Sunday of about the fifties, did something towards making the day a little less penitential for the mid-Victorians workers; but my memories of Sunday in the London of my childhood show only how small that something was, and how deadly the day must have been before he wrote. To-day, as I say, it is not yet the day of full freedom that it might be, but it is sufficiently cheerful to make a few aged hands rise in horrified condemnation. In my childhood one was taken to church at least once a day; and for the rest one could amuse oneself with bound volumes of *Sunday At Home, Good Words* and *The Leisure Hour,* or the horrific *Paradise Lost* of Doré. Comic papers were barred; indeed, anything amusing was barred, even such dull table-games as Snakes-and-Ladders or Word-Making. I wonder what a ten-year-old of to-day would say to such restrictions? Nothing, I expect. He would just ignore them and give Public Enemy No. 1 clear indication as to where he got off.

The pioneer in the demand for a sensible Sunday for the masses was the National Sunday League, which at its inception had to face sharp antagonism. But by its gradual enlightenment of public opinion it has been able to increase and widen its early activities in the way of concerts in town and cheap trips to sea and country, and to win general support for its efforts towards a full and free use of the rest-day. Instead of mooning stiffly up and down the local High Street, and creating for it the term "Monkeys' Parade," boy and girl workers can now get out by cheap tickets to the country, and, when they get there, they can find refreshment places open to serve them. Others can keep the whole Sunday in the fields by going off for Saturday-to-Monday walks. Still others get the car out and go exploring. These outlets, once possible only to a few, are now possible to millions. Many working-people now own family cars--second-hand things, bought for ten pounds, and sometimes less--and Sunday for them, instead of being what it was for their fathers--a day of lead--is a day of pagan refreshment, which can be nearer to spiritual refreshment than some sects imagine. Most of them probably are not capable of spiritual exercises, and, that being so, they are receiving just as much personal enrichment from the mere sight of flowers and hills as if they perfunctorily sat through a service.

Indeed, perhaps more, for when I compare a London Sunday crowd of forty years ago with a London Sunday crowd of to-day, I notice that the old grumpiness, which was an adjunct of the Sunday streets, has disappeared. People look and are more pleasant in manner and lighter in tone. If they are not healthier--and some doctors declare they are not--at least they radiate that air which we associate with health, and on the spiritual side I do not perceive that they fall below their fellows of the past. Those who observe the day in the old formal way also look happier than they did; more alert, more open-faced, more talkative. Everywhere one notes more spontaneous kindness and less benevolence. We of to-day have many more worries than our grandfathers had, but we are more resilient and adaptable in dealing with them.

Many factors have helped in this, but the strongest, I think, is our new way of spending Sunday. In the past the mass of the people were cheerful during the week, and had to be miserable on Sunday, thus cancelling the spirit of the week. To-day Sunday comes as a culmination of the week's cheerfulness, a day of active and conscious recreation which gives people a warm and companionate attitude to their fellow-creatures. I remember that somewhere about 1904, when cars were displacing carriages among the wealthy, Marie Corelli wrote a solemn onslaught on "The Motoring Sunday." It was a grim picture of the depravity of High Society, which, instead of attending church and promenading in Hyde Park after church, thus setting a delectable example to the lower ranks, went out to the air and sky in those new infernal machines, with Satan at the wheel. It foreshadowed the end of everything. One would like to know what she would have thought of the present Sunday, with all its innocent amusements, and with the roads crowded with the cars not only of the rich, but of the poor.

To us of to-day her attitude seems inexplicable, but at that time it was common, and even now, in certain odd corners, one may find it. Attitudes, however, are useless against the spirit of an age. Nothing can thwart the operation of a spirit, and within the last forty years it has manifested itself to the point where people may spend their Sunday in almost any way they please without being regarded as moral lepers. They may spend it in the open air of the country or the coast, or, if they possess a machine, they may spend it literally in the air. To the poorer people who are confined to town the spirit of the age has given concerts, tea-shops with music and song, boxing-matches, games in the parks, and, in the evening, picture-palaces, fun-fairs, pin-table saloons and dancing. Others of more means may have dancing and cabaret at their favourite restaurant or night club and, in a semi-secret, "subscription" way, theatres. They can enjoy all these things and still be regarded by serious people as fit to introduce into an unspotted home.

One is constantly hearing, from the elderly, peevish complaints about the restrictions of London life, but most people of wide experience will, I think, agree with me that in no other city can one be so comfortable as in London. Certain of the Sunday restrictions may be irksome and, to some people, irrational, but they are trifles compared with the Sunday restrictions operating upon the people of Edinburgh, Glasgow, Cardiff, Melbourne, Adelaide, and the capital cities of some American States. As to the ideal "freedom" which is popularly supposed to be the lot of the people of European countries, it scarcely bears examination. The illusion of French freedom particularly persists, but if you press the upholders of it closely enough you find that it resolves itself into the fact that you can get drinks in Paris at any hour, and that in London you can't. This fact so overwhelms them that they can see nothing else; yet even a brief consideration will show that as between London and other capitals there can be little doubt as to which city gives its citizens most freedom. If these Paris devotees attempted to address a meeting in Paris with all the freedom of the Hyde Park Sunday afternoon orators, they would find their meeting charged and dispersed, and themselves under arrest. You can walk about London, if you wish, with your belt filled with knives and daggers, and, so long as you walk peaceably, you will meet no trouble. You would not be allowed to go far in Paris with that make-up. In any London public place, restaurant, bar, railway-carriage, theatre, you may say what you like of England and the English and their government, and nothing happens. In Paris any such comments, spoken in the wrong café, would mean a riot of which you would be the centre. In London you may take a girl of respectable middle-class family, to whom you are not engaged, to dinner and a theatre or dance, and deliver her home in the early morning. You cannot do that in Paris. The bourgeois French are really more prudish than the English; their god is still *comme il faut*. What happens behind closed doors, or on the stage, is nobody's business, but in public their rules are stiffer than those of Jane Austen's middle-class. In London the young worker may lounge on the grass of Hyde Park or Green Park with his girl, and kiss her if he wishes, and public opinion is not disturbed. Let him try that little freedom in the Luxembourg or the Tuileries gardens. Let anybody, in short, live for twelve months in Paris, and then see what he has to say about the glories of Paris liberty and the grandmotherly restrictions of London.

From the advertisements in the daily press I fancy that public pleasure for the mass of Londoners must have increased ten-fold in the three decades of this century. Besides the inescapable picture-palace, you have dance-halls, whist-drives, greyhound stadiums, boxing, wrestling, ice-rinks, roller-rinks, fun-arcades, sun-bathing by the Serpentine, open-air theatres, public golf-courses and tennis-courts, and cabaret, which is to be had not only in the West End, but in a mild form in the suburban public-houses and tea-shops. There is also the private club, which is to be found in hundreds in west and central London, and in almost every suburb. All these amusements may in these days be had by people of quite humble means. For such people in my childhood there was very little. There were, of course, theatres and music-halls, and cricket and football, but most of the entertainment which is now general existed for particular groups. When my Aunt Jane was taking me about there was no very wide choice. I recall Hengler's Circus, where the Palladium now stands; the Royal Aquarium, near Parliament Street, which was an assembly of side-shows with a music-hall bill as the main feature; the Egyptian Hall, Piccadilly, where one saw Maskelyne and Cooke's entertainment; Mdme. Tussaud's; the Crystal Palace; and the St. James' Hall, now covered by the Piccadilly Hotel, where the Moore & Burgess minstrels had an annual season. And there was the glory of Earl's Court and its Big Wheel, and Buffalo Bill's Wild West show. That is all that the icebound album of the Old World affords me. There were other amusements, I know, but they were not available to people with narrow purses. For us there were these things--and the streets, whose coloured life, as I have said, perhaps compensated for the lack of other public pleasures.

When I tell children of to-day about the hours of delight we spent at those places, and what we saw and what we did, I can see from their faces that they are suffering one more pang of kindly contempt for the naïve pleasures of those who were born before they were. But we did have those hours and they did yield delight; as much delight as Wembley yielded to the children of 1924. Every age has its standard by which the spirit of wonder is excited. There was a time when Rosherville

Gardens with their grottoes and statuary could excite wonder. There was an earlier time when Vauxhall Gardens with their few hundred fairy-lamps dazzled the Society of their age. There was a time when the marble tea-shops which young people of to-day take for granted would have been the objects of excursions by the best people. Escalators are now an every-day feature of our Tube stations. I first saw this invention at the Royal Aquarium, where it was a centre of interest. It served no purpose there; it was a side-show, and you paid a penny to go up and down the "moving-staircase." Friends of mine have told me that when Matisse visited New York he couldn't be kept away from Roxy's cinema. Yet ten years from now, when Roxy and Radio City magnificence is as common as escalators, people will be wondering why they were impressed either to admiration or to hollow laughter. Give people something good, and they are delighted. Give them something better, and they not only find it better, but become contemptuous of the good thing that once afforded them delight. Though it sometimes happens that somebody, years later, revives the contemned old thing, and everybody finds it again delightful.

London, of course, however large its stock of public pleasure, will never have the holiday feeling of some of the cities of southern Europe. Its essential character through the ages has been always strong and deep and business-like. But this present London, despite the bad times, is wearing its strength and depth with easy shoulders. One sees everywhere more movement, more light, more air and more outdoor living. Restaurants, not only in the West End, but in the City too, have discarded their old Gothic heaviness of menu and decoration. The boudoir has displaced the baronial hall. Simpler diets have brought simpler and gayer fittings. Social London is not now the static jelly it once was. It is fluid, and is navigable by all sorts of interesting craft. All this reflects the new tone of life. London at any time has always reflected the spirit of that time, and the present lightening and blossoming of the town's life is a civic expression of the desire for a cleaner, fuller life for everybody, and a more seemly setting for it.

It was a general movement, but some credit for the brightening of outdoor life is due to Mr. George Lansbury for the example he set by his work on the London parks. It is odd that they should have waited so long for somebody to see their possibilities and use them to true advantage. The people of the past appear to have thought that it was sufficient to have an open space and plant it with formal beds, and cut walks through it, and set a brass band performing in it twice a week. That was a Park, and the stiffness of it matched the stiff word. In my childhood memories the word is associated with all varieties of stiffness. One was taken for stiff walks in the Park on stiff Sunday evenings. One went along stiffly-cut paths bordered by beds of stiff flowers, and paraded by people as stiff as oneself, though looking much stiffer. You were in a Park, and its stiff atmosphere sensibly changed you from what you had been in the street, five minutes before you entered it. During the war we made many jokes about the German *verboten,* but when I think of the parks of my childhood I think first of "Keep Off . . ." "Do Not . . ." and similar injunctions. No wonder we walked stiffly.

George Lansbury changed all that. He gave the children real playgrounds, sand-pits, and lakes and boats to themselves. He gave the adults a bathing-beach around the Serpentine--Lansbury's Lido, as it came to be called--and made the parks a riot of blossom. Most valuable of all, he contrived to enliven their tone and to infuse them with a real spirit of pleasure-garden which reacts upon the people in brighter faces and happier steps. All sorts of amenities were added or improved under his benign rule, and since the spirit he introduced has continued to flourish, it is now possible, thirty-three years after the death of Queen Victoria, for the Londoner to do as his grandfather did in the puritanical Victorian days--take a glass of wine or beer in at least one of the London parks.

I do not know how the myth of the puritanical Victorians arose, but lately it has been firmly fixed in the public mind by critics and novelists of the lifelong-undergraduate type, who seem to have been in search of a theme on which to display their undergraduate smartness. Being funny about the Victorians became the new literary sport. You didn't pin yourself to facts; you just wrote "out of your own head." These men, indeed, whose books have enjoyed during the last few years a vast sale among the non-studious, can have read little more social history than their readers. For had they made even a cursory survey of the popular press and popular amusements of the age, and looked half an inch below the bourgeois surface, they would have realised that their self-conceived notions of its primness and puritanism were wholly at fault, and that their fun-poking had scarcely anything to rest upon. The odd thing about these books is that, written in the nineteen-twenties and thirties, they are really a case of a distinctly black pot of prudery and repression making charges of blackness against an aluminium kettle of honesty and freedom. Those who do study London life of the mid-Victorian period know that whatever the life of the Court may have been, the life of the people was Anything But. It was an age of coarse and foolish amusements in which all classes joined, but it differed from ours in that they were pursued *openly*. Really, any charge of sham rectitude and humbug can more justly be brought against our own age than against the Victorians, for those same coarse and foolish amusements are still being pursued, but furtively and out of sight.

London under Victoria was as candidly and carelessly unmoral as it was under the Regency. A brief study of the less-guarded Society memoirs of the sixties and eighties will disclose this, and a study of the popular press will show that it was openly recognised and taken for granted. The press, in those supposedly strict days, was much freer than it is to-day. It could publish almost anything, and did. There was no conspiracy of silence about abuses and scandals, as there is to-day. It is we who do just what these modern critics accuse the Victorians of doing; it is we who maintain a hush-hush policy about disagreeable things. Those "hypocritical" Victorian editors did what no editor of these enlightened days can do; they told the truth about things and about people; even the most powerful people. They reported, in a quite casual way, things that no paper of to-day dare report, and as for comment, any editor of to-day who published comments half as free as those which George R. Sims was publishing in the seventies, would find himself in serious trouble.

Where *did* this absurd legend of prim and prudish Victorians have its beginning? It must have begun with somebody who had observed only provincial life, for London life, as I say, claimed and enjoyed licence to be what it chose. There were few laws against indulgence; the town was open all night; drinks and drugs were easily to be had; and the most secret amusements of to-day were available in the open. Certain queer doings, which we like to regard as "Modern" and "Freudian" had, each of them, somewhere in Victorian London, its temple; and what they didn't know about those things we haven't yet learnt. There is an amusing little work which may sometimes be found in secondhand book-shops, and of which I once saw a copy. It throws an interesting light on the real life of that age. It was a pocket-volume, dated 1851, the year of Albert's Great Exhibition; and it bore this title-page:

The Swell's Night Guide

to

The Great Metropolis

Displaying the Saloons; the Paphian Beauties;

the Chaffing Cribs; The Introducing Houses,

the French Houses, etc.

by

The Lord Chief Baron

It was the kind of book that, since Harman and Thomas Dekker, has appeared every half-century or so; a companion to Ned Ward's *London Spy* and Pierce Egan's *Life in London* and Westmacott's *English Spy;* except that each of these somewhat unkempt authors could have given this Victorian a lesson in seemliness and reticence. Not that there is anything in it that would shock a sensible person, and obviously nothing that shocked the supposedly susceptible Victorians; only gossip about things that people in those days accepted much more calmly than modern authority accepts them. It only says openly to its Victorian readers the kind of thing that intellectual novelists of this emancipated age have to print privately.

The editor, the "Lord Chief Baron," was a man named Renton Nicholson, well known to students of nineteenth-century life. He kept various taverns and hotels in London, and was the inventor of the successful Judge-and-Jury Trials, held nightly at one of his houses, the "Garrick's Head" in Bow Street. These were mock trials of imaginary divorce cases and unsavoury criminal cases. The judge was Nicholson himself; the jury was empanelled from his customers; and out-of-work actors played counsel and witnesses. They did it so well that, by contemporary report, they drew "all London." The whole object of this parody of a court was to elicit improper evidence and point it with improper comment; and these shows, which matched any entertainment devised by Sedley or Rochester, were publicly performed and regularly patronised by "the nobility and gentry" and most other classes throughout the second decade of the Age of Staid Propriety. Encouraged by their success, Nicholson went further, and introduced an exhibition of *Poses Plastiques,* which describe themselves. These were publicly advertised, admission one shilling, and were shown twice daily, and they had a long and profitable run before any protest was made against them. The "Baron" wrote of these shows, and of their reception by his patrons, in terms that, to a reader of this polite era, are almost embarrassing.

His Guide opened with a Preface on the twin joys of Bacchus and Venus, and then went on to describe the various night-resorts of London, high and low, and the individual tastes for which they catered. It ended with a directory of the names and addresses of the most noted women of the town, and comments upon the peculiar attractions of each. The principal all-night house, in tone and price, was the Royal Saloon, Piccadilly. It was famous for its cuisine, its cellar, and its women. The women were personally invited by the management, and no others were allowed to enter. The "Baron," I remember, found it a "somewhat scandalous" place, and if this widely experienced Victorian found it "somewhat scandalous" in comparison with some of the extraordinary "Introducing Houses" which he so freely and casually described later in the book, then it must have been a house that would have sent the broad-minded Watch Committees of 1934 into a swoon. Other prominent all-night houses of the West End were the "Baron's" own Garrick's Head; the Coal Hole, the Finish, the New Crockford's, the Elysium, the Windmill Saloon, and the Adelphi Shades. Across the river were a score of others, among them the New Inn, the Surrey Coal Hole, the Victoria Saloon, the Jim Crow, and Astley's Wine and Supper Rooms. There were also the saloons and foyers of the theatres, which were public rendezvous of a kind against which the Empire Promenade of the nineties was a Dorcas Meeting.

In all these Victorian night-resorts, those of fashion and those of the working classes, supper entertainments, not then made exotic by the word cabaret, were a regular feature; indeed, no tavern could hope to attract custom without an entertainment. Judging by the Guide's descriptions, each place appears to have afforded the spectacle of Victorian unfortunates behaving with all the free manners of the modern world of fashion--smoking, drinking, and painting their faces. The proverb about luxury is true, but so also is its converse. The deportment of the Victorian unfortunate is now the deportment of the respectable, and cabaret, which in 1851 was everybody's evening treat, is now the luxury of the few who are willing to pay its excessive price. The kind of cabaret they offered was mainly in the key of the master of the art, this "Baron"--disgusting, but open and frank, and perhaps less acid in its effect than the half-hearted smirks at impropriety offered by the cabaret entertainers of our London of to-day.

 The matter and style of the book might be described as a gale which leaves scarcely a wrack behind of that prim public life which the smart historians have offered to us as typical of the Victorian age. In his attitude to what the present-day prudishly labels "complexes" and "inhibitions," he was what Fleet Street calls "fearless" and "straight from the shoulder"; only he didn't know that he was. In those dark days, before short hair and cocktails and freedom and sincerity, and all the other blessings of the nineteen-thirties, they had neither the prudery that is easily shocked nor the prudery that delights to shock. Mid-Victorian women enjoyed the Mazeppa performance of Adah Isaacs Menken, and talked as bluntly as their men about the facts of life. It was only a small section--the petty bourgeois--who cultivated the "refined" attitude, and the blind eye to the human functions, and "genteel" amusements. It was only those papers produced "for the home" which called trousers "unmentionables," and depicted young men who smoked cigars on Sundays as on the road to the devil. The majority of the people held a John Blunt attitude to facts, where we of to-day are so self-conscious about our recognition of them that we become pop-eyed at meeting them and almost juvenile in showing everybody that we have been introduced. Our newspapers claim to treat all aspects of life in their columns, but most of them, I think, would shy at the "Baron's" utterances; I doubt if even those papers published on the Lord's Day would allow him to be quite as "fearless" as the Victorian age allowed him to be. He was most typical of his age, as it really was, in the section where he described prominent women of the town, and their manners and accomplishments in what he rather extravagantly called their private lives. I remember thinking at the time that it read like an auctioneer's address at a bloodstock sale.

But I will make the smart historians a present of one point for their case. In one spot of the book he did conform to their conception of his age. In a paragraph of blunter statement about certain matters than any "privately-printed" modern novelist has yet achieved, he wanted to use the word damned. He printed it "d----d."

A minor effect of the recent increase in the stock of public pleasure, both week-day and Sunday, may by some be regretted. It has made us forget the gracious art of lotus-eating. People have now so many things to "do" that they are like children in a toyshop. You cannot get them to sit down. The idea has got hold of us that action in itself--any action--is virtuous, and that idleness is shameful. We constantly talk of the need in public life for "men of action." It doesn't matter what tomfool things the man of action does, or what kind of muddle he creates; he is still, in the modern opinion, superior to the calm man who waits for things to take their course. He is one of the current heroes, and the majority of people take him for a model. Even those who have no need to be busy feel that they must simulate busy-ness, and the majority of the leisured classes know no more what to do with themselves and their time than the suddenly unemployed. All they can do with their blessed gift of leisure is to debase it into scampering action--in dancing, golfing, calling on friends, going to parties, telephoning, "running" something. Those who really have work to do make that work their commander and themselves its slave. Men in the past did as much work as is done to-day, but they were able always to adjust themselves to a little lotus-eating. To-day they are incapable of reclining; the glorification of work has poisoned their systems. For work and busy-ness are as stealthy and as potent in their dreadful effects as morphine. Once you get the habit you can't stop. It gives no pleasure, but you must go on. We see constantly the spectacle of men who have made fortunes in business and cannot retire. The poor creatures simply do not know how to do nothing. I have had specimens of them at my three-hour lunches, which begin about one o'clock and dawdle into tea-time. They were ill at ease. They kept fidgeting and murmuring about Getting Back or Getting Along or Busy Day. They shook their heads at my "wasting" of time.

Scarcely any little office of our daily round is free from this poison of snap and pep. Our bath and our shave are perhaps the last occasions left to us for wallowing in leisure, and these are in danger. You cannot have a leisurely bath in a hotel unless you book a suite; and advertisers are constantly offering us some new shaving cream which will do the job in fifteen seconds. Dinner, when I was a boy, was dinner. To-day it is a race against time. The gentle vespers of the table are interrupted by the clamant theatre or movie, and often what might have been a dinner to remember is ruined by the anti-digestive rush to an inane first-night. Only in a corner here and there, in the little homes of artists and scholars, and among those who follow angling (one outdoor recreation which has so far escaped "brightening") is leisure cherished and enjoyed. There the nineteenth-century models of those two futile insects, the ant and the bee, have no shrine. The models, if any, are those of the moth on the sunny wall and the cat on the cushioned chair. The cat has a far better instinct for the art of living than the general run of humans. It works with zest when work is necessary, and when there is no reason for work it takes its ease hour after hour. Through indolence it grows in grace and self-content, while we, with our constant action, grow nerve-ridden, tight-lipped and hard-eyed. All because of this doctrine that work and busy-ness are of themselves admirable, and that even such a beautiful thing as leisure must be "used." One does not put butterflies and flowers to the base purposes of "use." One enjoys them, which is what one should do with leisure.

Much of the economic trouble from which we are now suffering is due to this very vice of work. If we had done less work we shouldn't have reached this pass. As for the old warning that Satan finds some mischief for idle hands to do, one can only retort that if the man had used his eyes he would have seen that it isn't true. Idle hands won't allow themselves to be disturbed by any suggestion, not even from Satan, of "doing" things. Nine-tenths of the mischief wrought in this world is wrought by the active hands. It is for them that Satan is so zealous in finding things to do, and it is they who should be reproved and the indolent who should be applauded. Our present gods--Isaac Watts and Samuel Smiles--should be demolished, and we should set up in their place those gentle guides to true living--Izaak Walton and Quintus Horatius.

In some degree the decay of lotus-eating may be traced to women. I believe that men, left to themselves, would still cultivate idleness. It is their women who prod and upbraid them with suggestions of sin. It is they who compel them to Go Places and Do Things, and who break up the lovely still-life of leisure with comminations. Under women's urge, plus the glorification of work, they have become slaves to activity. They are the creatures of an age of movement. Most of it is purposeless movement, but it is as necessary to this generation as the movement on his wheel is necessary to the dormouse.

Still, those of us who dislike it must console ourselves with the reflection that anything we say has been said by every generation. Life is never fast enough for the active and never sufficiently tranquil for the lovers of the lotus. Ever since London began there have been complaints of the hot pace of London life. Lydgate complained of it; Stubbes complained of it; William Langland complained of it. Throughout English literature, stage by stage, you may find this plaint of the whirl of London, the quest for pleasure, the rush, the noise. Smollett's Matthew Bramble let off his spleen against the turmoil and fever of London life in the mid-eighteenth century, in terms almost exact to the terms used by moralists about the London of last year. There are always some who are a little behind the contemporary beat; slack or querulous members of the orchestra who *will* make their entry two bars late and then complain that the others are rushing it. Every generation has its beat, always an acceleration of that which preceded it; and those who were contemptuous of their grandfather's complaints about the nerve-racking pace of London in the eighties are in their turn complaining of the pace which their grandsons find easy and necessary. And fifty years hence those grandsons will be making similar complaint of the pace of the times, and will look back to the quiet, leisurely days of the nineteen-thirties.

One feature of the times which has always agitated the elders is the dance. To-day, as always, while the young are enjoying modern dances and modern dance-bands, the elders, true to type, are raising peevish objections to their ugliness and noise. They didn't like the Cake Walk; they didn't like the Turkey Trot or the Bunny Hug; they don't like the Fox Trot or the Charleston, and they can't do the Tango. They consider the Rumba vulgar, and could hardly bring themselves to mention the Black Bottom. They knew the graceful waltz, and can't understand why anybody wants anything else; forgetting, or not knowing, that Byron--even Byron--found the waltz vulgar. There are still to be found people who consider any kind of modern dancing vulgar, and public dance-halls as ante-rooms to something so dreadful--or perhaps so vague--that they cannot give a name to it.

The Palais de Danse and the professional partner, now a regular feature of London life in all classes, are developments of this century which would have made my Aunt Jane dislodge her spectacles by over-lifted eyebrows. Thirty years ago dancing *could* be had by ordinary, small-pocket people, but it was not as now a constant every-evening affair, and there were no halls solely devoted to it. It was "got-up" on occasions, and everything was done to a formula. It was usually held in the "Assembly Rooms" of the suburb, and prices ranged from five shillings to threepence, according to the district. Among the well-to-do, dances were mostly held at home, though hotels were being more and more used. Dancing at dinner in the better restaurants was an insanity not then thought of. The *thé dansant* crept into the hotels about 1912, but the *diner dansant*, with dancing between courses, did not arrive until just after the war. By that time we had thrown away the tango, the seductive voice of Buenos Aires, and set up temples to the negroid Priapus. And had canonised the dance-band.

I can recall the time when hostesses who had engaged a band for their dance treated the leader of the band, believe it or not, with no more ceremony than they used to their butlers. They had hired him to perform a job, and they paid him for it, and that was that. They seldom knew his name nor cared whether he had one. Young men who wanted special dances played told him what they wanted, and at the end of the evening slipped him a sovereign or so. They did not nervously ask him if he would be so kind; they did not invite him to their bachelor party; they did not tell their friends that they knew him; they did not beg him to give them lessons. They would no more have thought of that than of asking the gas-fitter to give them lessons in gas-fitting. To-day he is just a little lower in esteem than Schnabel, and considerably higher than Caruso ever was. He and the gigolo are the lions of to-day's London scene; and it is possible that the fact that no dance-band leader has yet been knighted is causing some feeling in dance-band circles.

Byron, in the opening of "Don Juan," remarked that his wanting a hero was an uncommon want, when every month brought forth its own. In these times heroes are everywhere, all day and every day, and the favourites are those who supply public amusement. In one world the dance-band leader and the gigolo are rulers, but in other worlds they are run pretty close by the odds-on greyhound and those men with the queer names who seek self-slaughter on the motor-cycle dirt-track. My Aunt Jane lived long enough to see Hengler's Circus turned into a "real ice" skating-rink. She thought it dangerous, physically and morally; she would not like any niece of hers to go there. Skating in the country was one thing, but skating in town . . . she understood there were instructors--handsome young men. It didn't seem quite right for young ladies to be escorted round the rink by strange young men. . . . I am glad she did not live to see her grand-nieces ogling the vacuous eyes of a crooner, to see her middle-aged niece languishing in the arms of a professional partner, or to see young girls falling on the muddy neck of the dirt-track hero.

The young London girl now goes everywhere and goes alone if she wishes. No public amusement is barred to her. You see her at the race-course, the greyhound-course, the dirt-track, the boxing-match, the wrestling-match, the football-match, the night club (both town and riverside), the palais de danse, the smoking-rooms of tea-shops, the brasserie, and even in your own club. You can't keep her out of anything. When I was a youth a frequent advertisement in popular magazines was that of a firm offering detachable billiard-tables. It was headed "Keep Your Boys at Home." I never discovered why it was thought desirable to keep boys at home, but there may be many people to-day who would think that course desirable for girls. The girls might not like it, but in these days of the constant mingling of the sexes there come, even to the most companionate men, occasional hours when they would like to be apart from women. And there are not three places where they can be.

A necessary adjunct of all entertainment is the restaurant, and as public entertainment has developed so the restaurant has developed with it. Few people, I imagine, of the eighteen-eighties can have foreseen the enormous growth of this industry over the whole face of London. It comes almost next to transport as one of the visible factors of change in the life and habits of the people. To young people of to-day a London without popular restaurants to which anybody can go for any sort of meal, is almost inconceivable; yet fifty years ago it had very few, if any, of that sort. It had, of course, plenty of restaurants, but they were specialised. The West End had a number of imposing restaurants and supper-rooms and lounges, and the foreign refugees who had settled around Leicester Square, and were beginning the Soho of to-day, had opened restaurants for their compatriots. Neither of these groups was available to the ordinary person--one by reason of expense, the other by reason that these foreign cafés *were* foreign and did not then seek general patronage. The middle-class restaurants and "dining-rooms" to be found in the Strand, Covent Garden and Haymarket catered almost wholly for men, and family groups lunching or dining out usually patronised hotels. For ordinary people there was the tavern--a thing distinct from the public-house. For people of the artisan class there was nothing but the grubby coffee-shop or "cook-shop." In the suburbs, such catering as existed was done by an Italo-Swiss café ("from Gatti's").

In the City there were but two kinds of restaurant. Women had not at that time invaded its offices, and at lunch-time it was concerned only with men. The employers patronised the chop-house--William's, Thomas's, Baker's, Pimm's, the Bay Tree, Birch's--or such taverns as the London and the Dr. Butler's Head; the employed patronised the cook-shop. Women were not seen in these places, nor, as I say, in the more central places--Cheshire Cheese, Simpson's, Keene's, Gow's, Snow's, Stone's, Carr's. The male attitude to women in those days was distinctly Sultanic. But it was the last flicker of that attitude. Even as Abdul was being shorn of his prerogatives by the Powers, so was the English male being forced by his women-kind to forego his Sultanism, and admit them to his snuggeries.

In the late eighties and early nineties, that period of New manifestations, a few people observed this breaking out of women and the lack of suitable catering for the extra floating population, and set out to meet it. The tea-shop arrived. It began cautiously. But it soon found that, unlike so many innovations, it did not have to create a want for itself. It actually did, as many innovations falsely claim to do, fill a want which had been long-felt, not only by women but by numbers of men of the City-office class, who were tired of the eating-house and the public-house. Within a few years it bred and multiplied until it was represented all over the City and in all the popular streets. To-day, of course, under the control of two or three firms, it is everywhere, and in different forms and styles it caters for everybody, from the tea-and-bun to the table d'hôte dinner.

Many explanations of the easy mixing, if not levelling, of the classes which has happened in the last fifty years, have been put forward, among them popular education, the decay of the professions, the extension of the franchise, the Social Conscience, and so on. None of these, I think, had much to do with it. Political enactments certainly did not, and could not. The chief factors in the matter I would name as the Tube, the cheap car, and the tea-shop. Before the Tube arrived, the masses travelled by tram and bus--and only the masses. Nobody of any social position used either; they belonged to the workers. When the masses needed refreshment they used their fixed retreats--eating-houses, coffee-shops and sausage-shops; and only themselves were seen there. To-day, people of all classes use the Tube and the tea-shop. In certain districts one may regularly see lawyers, artists, writers, bankers and Whitehall figures taking coffee in the tea-shop. These places have become the equivalent of the European café, where you may meet anybody and everybody. In the past one would have wondered to see Judges of the High Court, or Counsel, taking refreshment in the people's refreshment places, or riding in the people's conveyances. They may often be seen to-day. Similar-sounding terms (coffee-shop and tea-shop) have a wide social gap between them. The former is still the Good Pull Up for Carmen; the latter an affair of marble and gilt, efficiency and cheapness, which at odd times is found convenient by people of all sorts. So with the Tube and the motor-bus; they are beneath nobody's dignity.

The tea-shop of to-day is the twentieth-century form of the eighteenth-century coffeehouse--another term which, despite similarity, indicates something widely different from the coffee-shop. Everybody may use it, and almost everybody does. Looking around the company of one of these places at coffee-time, it is difficult to judge from appearances whether a man is a clerk, a controller of a big business, a novelist, a motor-coach driver, or whether he keeps a stall in a market-place or holds a portfolio in the Cabinet. Accent is still some clue, but even here it gives no clear direction. The fine accent may come from the coach driver and the ugly accent from the powerful business man. The man who, by old standards, looks as though he kept a stall may be one of England's four outstanding poets; and the man who, by old standards, looks as though he were in the Diplomatic Service, is probably a chorus man in a musical show. Outward distinctions, as I have said, are rapidly being obliterated in all departments and occasions of London life, but there is no place like the tea-shop for making everybody the lowest common denominator of a crowd. It is now as constant a feature of London life as the public-house used to be, and there is scarcely any shopping street within the six-mile radius where it is not to be found.

The company at these places is representative of the note of the district in which each is situated. In the City the company is clerks and perhaps junior partners. In Bloomsbury it is students. In Oxford Street it is women shoppers and shop-assistants. Around the railway termini it is travellers of any and every sort. In Fleet Street it is journalists and young barristers. In Whitechapel it is jewellers and furriers. In Hatton Garden it is pearl and diamond dealers and their assistants. During the evening hours they are used mainly by the lonely; people who have no homes, but "lodge" somewhere. You may see there the old book-keeper who sits every evening at the same table at a given minute of each evening, and never varies his austere meal or the newspaper that he reads column by column. There are men of his sort who have sat regularly at their tea-shop table these twenty-five years; characters, some of them. In the past, when I was one of those evening customers, I came to know, by use of the same table, uncelebrated philosophers; grey-haired, unpublished poets; apostles of strange religions; and a few nice old fellows with no special hobbyhorse. I listened to plans for the reconstruction of society; to expositions of Swedenborg; and to discourses on matters of which I would otherwise have remained in ignorance--such as the æsthetic thrill of philately, the antiquities of Kensal Green, the symbolism of chess, the significance of blue in primitive painting.

People of this sort are not found in the more gorgeous development of the tea-shop. The company in those places is not there for the purpose of getting necessary food. It is there for warmth, light, rich carpets, ornate walls, music, the surge of people. It is there for refreshment of nerves and spirit. It is there for its share of splendour, which these places have democratised. The fastidious among us may wish that it had been done in some less flamboyant style, but who are we among so many?

Side by side with this tea-shop growth, and its development into palaces and pavilions, has gone the growth of the proprietary restaurant. Since the brothers Gatti opened the first large café-restaurant, and were followed on a similar scale by Nicol and others, it has spread rapidly and regularly, year by year. The innovation of mansion-flats, the gradual decay of formal domestic cooking, and the new pleasure which people found in restaurant life, gave it a sharp impetus, and to-day it is one of the major London industries.

In the nineties came the fashion of "those little places," and Soho's fortune was made. The little places provided new food, more varied menus, "different" surroundings, a vivacious atmosphere, and deft service;

all at prices little higher than those of the eating-houses and below those of the chop-house. At the beginning of the century, as I have said, one could find between Shaftesbury Avenue and Oxford Street a dozen places serving a four-course bourgeois dinner at a shilling, and many more serving dinner at one-and-six; while at half-a-crown you could eat well, and at five shillings you could dine. The Dieppe, now vanished from Old Compton Street, lived for many years on its shilling dinner, and was packed every evening, and the half-crown dinners of the more glossy places, frequently of seven courses, were so well known among the slender-pocketed that if you were not there early you could not find a table. Across Oxford Street, in Charlotte Street, you could find, as now, similar places, though mostly German and Swiss, and many of these served dinner at even less than a shilling. These were quite small places, where the customers knew one another, and Madame knew them all, and conversation was general between tables and between Madame and clients. You dined there almost as one of the family.

Those Soho places came and went. A few of them were fixtures, and some which are in flourishing operation to-day have had over forty years of prosperity. But others had short lives, or moved about from street to street. You would know them for two years. Then, after an absence, you would go along one night, and they weren't there. But you would hear of a new place down the street, just opened, and you would become one of its occasionals until it, too, disappeared, and you would learn that its waiter (service in the smaller places was seldom plural) had opened a place of his own in Greek Street or Frith Street. Or you would seek a favourite restaurant at its old address, and find it gone, but would learn that it was flourishing in a new home three streets away. Or you would find the old place, but you would find that a change had come over it which meant finis for that café so far as you were concerned; you would find that it had been discovered by the smart and semi-smart. And you would look about for a new place with the right intimate atmosphere, and help to make its owner's fortune until he, too, was discovered by the wrong people.

The war, as I have said, gave Soho a boom period, and it was during this period that it lost its old personal note and became anybody's place. The suburbs and the provinces invaded it, and the young officer from the small town proved his knowledge of London by exhibiting its cafés to his relations. It became self-conscious, and from doing a casual job in a casual but effective way, unaware that it was doing anything remarkable, it laid itself out to attract all London. It became a cult and performed its job with display and advertisement. But it is still one of the pleasantest quarters of the town, and it is unique in that within its small acreage one can eat with almost every country of the world. France, Italy, Switzerland, Germany, Spain, the Balkan states, Greece, Turkey, Palestine, Japan, America, Poland, Hungary, Armenia, Russia, China, India, Brazil--all are represented here. Only the

Scandinavian countries are missing. Their cafés you must seek in Rotherhithe.

As the Soho places come and go, so do the larger places. Many a restaurant in high fashion thirty years ago has disappeared. Others, while still alive, are prospering from a different clientièle. Others again, obscure in my youth, are now in favour. Among those that have gone in my time are the Globe, in New Coventry Street; the Continental, in Regent Street; the Gaiety, in the Strand; the Pall Mall, Les Gobelins, Pratti's in Whitehall, the St. James, and more whose names escape me. Yet despite all changes of taste and fashion, and all new arrivals, there are some which have gone on from decade to decade. Gatti's, the pioneer of café-restaurants, is still with us; also Verrey's, the Café Royal, Oddenino's, Romano's, Scott's, Prince's, Les Lauriers, Jules, and others which date back to the distant past. Notable and highly successful arrivals of the new generation are Sovrani's, Monseigneur, Quaglino's, Hungaria, Boulestin's, Bellometti's, the Ivy, and that restaurant frequented by the staff and artists of the B.B.C., the Bolivar.

Hotels, too, are favourites or victims of the whims of fashion. Many that once were world-famous have gone from the London scene within the last few years, and the "family" hotel is hardly represented at all. Ridler's has gone, and Morley's; the Golden Cross, the Tavistock, the Inns of Court, the Cecil, De Keyser's, the Salisbury, the Walsingham House, and the Grand--all of which seemed to be permanent landmarks of the streets. Yet others, many of them older than these, such as the Langham, Brown's, Batt's, the Berkeley, and Garland's, remain and prosper. The oyster bar alone in the refreshment world seems armoured against change, as though oysters conferred some spirit of permanence. White's, Driver's, Bennett's, Pimm's and Scott's flourish as when I first knew them.

The chop-house, solid and fixed as it seemed in the eighties, has suffered a thinning-out. But the three Simpson's survive, one in the Strand, another off Cheapside, and the third in St. Michael's Alley; also the George & Vulture, the Cheshire Cheese, Snow's and Stone's; and Birch's, though it has gone from Cornhill, is still Birch's in Old Broad Street. They are not today restricted to their former business of chop and steak. As the modern grill-room no longer restricts itself to grills, so these chop-houses are full-blossomed restaurants, with a double-fronted menu from smoked salmon to savoury and sweet. Let us hope they may stay with us yet awhile, for they are the only really *English* restaurants London has, and our only link with the dining habits of the past. They are the city's equivalent of the old inns of the countryside; visible factors in the continuity of London life. I am not moved by their "old-world" atmosphere; there is nothing "romantic" in dining at the chop-house, and at the same table, where your great-grandfather dined. But it is useful and pleasant in that it reassures you that there is no such thing as the past. There is only one long present, and we and our great-grandfathers are moments of it, making one of the changing company of that chop-house which survives us all.

The waiters of the many vanished City chop-houses were in a class by themselves. They had little in common with the dapper, ballerino waiters of the foreign cafés. They were grave, suave, and fatherly; something of the butler type. When they were deferential it was with the assured deference of a prince. They were Old Masters of their craft, who had the air of having begun their career when the chop-house was built, and of being as much a part of it as the old fireplace and the blue table-china. They were in a tradition which went back to Francis of the "Boar's Head," and through George of Ben Jonson's "Mitre" and the stout head-waiter of Tennyson's "Cock." And however aged they were--and my recollection is that they were all grey--it was correct to address them by Christian names--Henry, William, Charles, Fred. They were as deft in service as any of the Italians, but what mainly won my admiration was that in days before there were any schools for memory-training, they had memories which missed nothing. Any face they had once seen, any name they had once heard, any individual preference in food or drink, they remembered. Often I have gone as a stranger to a chop-house twice in a fortnight, and each time have ordered the same meal--say a chop, boiled potatoes, and a Guinness. Then there has been a gap of two months. Being in its neighbourhood at the end of the two months, I have gone again to that chop-house, and ordered of that same waiter a chop, boiled potatoes, and--"Yessir, and a Guinness?"

On affairs of the past they were reliable referees. Young men, disputing of this or that, could summon them to settle the argument. "When did Pomposo win the Gold Cup?" or "Who was the co-respondent in the Poodlechuck case?" or "What was the Benson case?" They would reflect for a moment; then, with a recitative of "Why, now, let me see--that'd be--" out would come the information. When those young men were suffering from last night, the Williams, Johns and Henrys could suggest right remedies, and accompany them with sage advice on how to manage an evening. They could advise them on the ways and wiles of women, and particularly on the ways and wiles of City adventurers. In times of stress they could come to the rescue with a loan. Many of them were more economically secure than numbers of their customers, but always, in the chop-house or when meeting in the street, the customer was the customer and they were waiters. They were the figures of an age, and that age has passed. But they are enshrined in its story. In their day men remembered them and talked of them in lonely places thousands of miles from London. I am told that in these days men in lonely places thousands of miles from London wear the old school tie and dress for dinner. That is another reason for regretting the chop-house; such barbarian customs as stiff shirts were never fostered on their sand and sawdust.

Since the war we have seen another kind of restaurant spring up all over London, mainly in side-streets of the central quarters. These places are in all points the opposite of the chop-house. They are run by women for women. They have no licence. They are usually of one room, furnished with slim chairs and with tables two-feet square intended to accommodate four people. They serve dainty lunches and bear some "whimsy" name out of children's books. So far as their food and service are concerned, they are good enough, but they lack the one thing that makes a restaurant, which is the restaurant *atmosphere.* They are just rooms where people feed, and their "dinky" furniture, paper-napkins, tiny tables, synthetic flowers, and their revealed efficiency and anxious attentiveness (which one should never be aware of) are all the opposite of what one evokes by the word restaurant. I prefer the revealed *in*efficiency??? and deformed organisation which one sometimes finds in a newly-opened foreign café, when Madame rates the waiter, and the waiter retorts to Madame, and the chef appears from below, and the trio, careless of the customers, engage in a match of recrimination. And then Madame announces to the first few customers, hoarsely and honestly and dramatically, that Everything Is Wrong, and how could she expect it to be Right with two such people as those? But it will be right to-morrow, *bien sûr.* However, as those places are intended chiefly for women, a man's views are not in place. The fact that they are successful and are constantly appearing proves that they supply a need and are appreciated. They make a pleasant change for the business-girl who is tired and who seeks a quiet place in preference to the over-crowded and rather noisy tea-shop. And perhaps, when they have been a part of the London scene for a few years more, they will develop their own atmosphere and patina, and in time found a tradition and become to women what the chop-house became to men.

There is one point which marks all restaurants of to-day from the restaurants of forty years ago, and that is over-crowding. With the increase of restaurants to meet the increase of London's daily and nightly population, we still seem to have too few. At the beginning of the century one could dine almost anywhere in comfort, but now every place, cheap or expensive, good or bad, is uncomfortably crowded. Hard times or prosperous times make little difference; wherever you go, at whatever time, the crowd has got there before you. In those days a restaurant could be only half-full (thus giving not only space to those who were there but the *sense* of spaciousness and ease) and still be commercially successful. To-day, apparently, commercial success is only attained when the place is jammed to capacity for both lunch and dinner, and tables are set twelve inches from each other. A bromidic utterance of my Aunt Jane's, when she was in town, was that the sight of the streets made you wonder where all the people came from. I don't care where the people come from, but whenever I enter a restaurant these days I have a deep desire that they would go back to wherever it is.

It is scarcely possible now to take even a drink in comfort. In the days before the war, bars, being open all day, were cool and comfortable places. Their custom was spaced out through some sixteen hours, and at no time were they crowded. One could sit at one's table in almost any lounge in the centre of town, as serenely as in one's own home; and even the ordinary public-house was much less flurried and rib-jamming than it is now. Strange as it sounds in these times, men used then to go into a public-house to seek a little peace away from the crowd. They could go to a wine-house for a ninepenny goblet of champagne as other people go to a cathedral. They could be sure of a retired seat and of room to move their arms. To-day, the world is with us soon and late, and during the restricted hours of opening it is almost futile to look for one of those "quiet" places of which London once had so many. All places seem to be popular and to have their constant crowd, and all hours are rush-hours. In the past, each London district had its set population during the day, varying only a little this way or that; but in these times of rapid transport people come to everywhere from everywhere, and all through the day the provinces and the suburbs fill up what used to be the thin hours and the unfertile spaces.

Apart from this matter of over-crowding, the London public-house or tavern of to-day is a much more seemly affair than its recent forerunner. Everywhere the old gilt and glass, frosted-mirror and mahogany gin-palace of the eighties and nineties, with its enclosed counters and heavy doors, is disappearing, and in its place we have a less ornate and more open structure. In place of the four penitential compartments we have imitation Tudor snuggeries. In the bars of a more expensive sort, the Long Bar, an American innovation of the nineties, has given place to open lounges and smoking-rooms. Most of these rebuilt places are fitted with cold-lunch bars, and drinks are more varied than they were forty years ago. American and French drinks are in favour, and the old cordials, which then were a feature of every London bar--shrub, clove, lovage, noyeau; and spruce beer--are seldom seen. In the suburbs, a recent development has been the family house, which is public-house, restaurant and tea-shop, all in one, with gardens and public rooms available to children as well as adults. But nobody seems to have found a new design for the public-house. All over central London one sees ugly old Victorian places rebuilt to a copy of Elizabethan or Stuart styles. Those styles were very well for the people of Elizabeth and the Stuarts, but they have nothing to do with the London of the nineteen-thirties, and when you find them set among new buildings of the latest northern concrete style, they are a foolish incongruity. If we must hark back for ideas, the late Georgian style would mix better with our current Scandinavian outlines; but why cannot we have our taverns as apt to the times as the new commercial buildings? Why do their designers inevitably think Tudor instead of thinking Le Corbusier?

While the old-style public-house of the later nineteenth century has gone or is going from central London, specimens of it are still to be found by the amateur of curiosities. He need only look in the near suburbs, the best ground being, I think, the south-eastern districts. There he will find many a saloon with the furniture and appointments of the eighties and nineties. He will find green "art" pots of aspidistras on walnut tables, horsehair chairs and lounges, and "art" overmantels. On the walls he will see coloured prints of Buller, Wauchope, Hector Macdonald. If he is lucky he will also see that once-popular print in which Lord Roberts figures in an unmartial and far from King's Regulations moment--"Can't You See I'm Busy?" A friend and myself used to "collect" these superannuated bars and make competition in our new additions. I once scored heavily by discovering a remote house with ancestral pictures of Sir Garnet Wolseley, and of the Last Stand at Isandlwana; but my friend drew level the next week by finding one with a presentation-plate of Stanley presuming he saw Dr. Livingstone and a steel engraving framed in old maple of The Rt. Hon. John Bright, M.P., Addressing The House. We have found saloon bars with chiffoniers and anti-macassars; with what-nots and rustic brackets, and artificial flowers under glass shades. Indeed, by careful scouting one can make a tour of time, via these public-houses, through various decades even into the sixties. There is a strong conservatism in some of these near suburbs. They live in a world of petrol and electricity and sun-parlours, and in that world they enjoy the benefits of these things. But in their own homes and their own minds they stay where they grew up, and they like their public-houses to reflect not antiquity but the time when the middle-aged of to-day were young. So they hold on to the walnut what-not, and see no reason for replacing it with steel chairs and chromium tables.

The changes that have operated upon most of London's amenities have operated also upon the club. The small, intimate club, with a limited membership, can hardly be run in these days without heavy loss, and many clubs, neither large nor small, have had difficult times since the war. The sudden economic slump led many men to abandon their clubs, but apart from hard times men do not find a club so necessary as they formerly did. Affairs for the engagement of time are now so profuse and so varied that large numbers have "no time" for a club. The growth of the restaurant, too, has robbed the club of one of the advantages it had when restaurants were few and formal; and it looks as though the club-life of which our elders talk with such enthusiasm is in danger of decay. The younger men certainly do not seem to take to it very keenly, in spite of the abolition of entrance-fees; they are more attracted by the Country Club, which is an institution of another colour--American, too.

Within my short time the club atmosphere also has suffered a change, or, as a specific atmosphere, disappeared. One has no longer the feeling of being in a secluded gathering. The dining-room, lounge and smoking-room of the average club to-day might equally be rooms in a good hotel. The purely masculine note also is gone. In most clubs, before the war, women could get no farther than the entrance-hall. To-day, almost all clubs have a room where members can entertain their ladies, and some, which once were limited to men, are now admitting women members. Thus, monastic hours are no longer possible, and all that men knew by the word "club" has gone into the common stock, and set them in the family atmosphere from which the original club was an intended escape. But a number of the older clubs of the St. James district have set a stout front against this innovation, and are still the preserve of the male; and I believe there is one other kind of club to which women have not yet penetrated--the cabmen's shelters, which became a cult with young poets of the nineties. They used them as night-clubs, and retired to them at four o'clock in the morning for eggs-and-bacon. Not because they wanted eggs-and-bacon at four o'clock in the morning, but because the bourgeois did not eat eggs-and-bacon in cabmen's shelters at four o'clock in the morning.

This habit has lately been revived in London since the coming of the all-night tea-shop and café. This all-night service supplied a real need--the need of the night-workers who, until then, could get refreshment only at the draughty coffee-stall, and not very good refreshment. But in addition to supplying a need it created one; it caught the custom of people who were not night-workers and who did not have to be about the streets at all hours. Ordinary people discovered that they liked having a meal at three o'clock in the morning, chiefly because they could get it. It was "fun." When these places were first opened, many people who had no reason for staying out deliberately stayed out; sometimes deliberately went out; and ate a meal which they did not want, just for the new sensation of sitting in a public café between midnight and six o'clock. The American supper-stand, an arrival of the last ten years, is a more resplendent kind of coffee-stall, offering a wider menu than the ham-rolls, hard-boiled eggs and gravelly cakes of the original stalls. They supply fried sausages, hot-dogs, apple fritters, sweet corn, and most of the snacks to be had at the delicatessen stores. Other night restaurants are the carmen's "caravanserai," usually set under arches or within vacant building lots. These are to be found not only in London, but on all the roads out of London; so far out that you find them set in hedgerows or at the corner of a meadow facing cross-roads, even as travellers found similar places four hundred years ago. On these roads also, some ten miles from the London boundary, are proper carmen's restaurants and carmen's hotels.

The road-houses on the London sections of the great main roads I have already mentioned. In the summer they do well with their all-night swimming-pools, and in the winter they do equally well with their dance-bands and badminton courts. They, too, have supplied a modern need; a need which the Londoner did not know until New York impregnated him with it; the need of "some place to go." It doesn't apparently matter what you find when you get there. The going is the thing, and anybody who can provide any reason or excuse for "going" somewhere is certain of a profit. Entertainment value is an almost incalculable factor, and those whose business it is to provide the Londoner with entertainment find him a creature of capricious tastes. Often the atmosphere of entertainment, if he has had to go to some trouble to reach it, pleases him more than its substance, and many of those who have sunk money in providing real entertainment have found that the Londoner prefers to put a shilling in a new kind of slot and get nothing, to handing a shilling over an everyday counter for a solid shillings-worth. Years ago I knew a small boy who was sent to a fair on a Bank Holiday, and given a shilling to spend. Among all the carefully-calculated and thrilling entertainments of that fair, this boy chose to spend his shilling on things that were part of his everyday. He bought himself two ice-creams and *four wash-and-brush-ups*. He was a typical Londoner.

STREETS

Attending last year a revival of that "heart-throbbing, domestic drama" of the sixties, "The Streets of London," I was moved by the title to compare the streets of Diamond Jubilee time with the streets of to-day. The streets of to-day are the streets I trod then, but how different in complexion and atmosphere! How much lighter, cleaner, brisker; how improved in visibility! The streets of the old London in wet weather always implied mud. Women crossed the street gingerly, with skirts lifted high. Even men went carefully, picking their steps here and there. The surfaces used then seemed to produce mud, and the horses' feet churned it and kicked it up, and the many wheels going over it corrugated each roadway with little hills of viscid mud. The street-orderlies were busy all day, if not with mud then with horse-droppings. With all their efforts, the streets were still not half so trim as they are to-day.

It was during the nineteen-noughts, if I remember rightly, that Bernard Shaw (or was it H. G. Wells?) made some comment on these conditions, and suggested that with the increased use of petrol Londoners would begin to realise that their streets might and could be as inoffensive to the sight and to the boots as the floors of their drawing-rooms. We have not quite reached that ideal, but the wholesale use of the car, the decline of horse-traffic (which agitation may in time completely ban from the main streets), and the new surfaces of our roadways, have helped us a good way towards it. Falling down when crossing the street on a wet day is not now the wreckage of your day which it was. You may get somewhat soiled, but a quick brush will put you right. Forty years ago you could only put yourself right by a complete external change.

That London was not only a London of mud, but a London of darker nights. It had its great glittering streets, but these were mainly in the central west. Away from the principal streets it was none too well lit. There were miles of sad streets, heavy houses and small, glimmering shops. One of the terrors of my childhood was those long, silent side-streets, with only a sickly lamp here and there, stretching into an infinity of murk and pathos. They added a grievous burden to the general sigh which is the breathing of all great cities. They seemed crowded with invisible presences and fears, and one turned from them to the light and movement of the main streets as to sanctuary. To-day one finds few of them in central London or even in the near suburbs. The most secluded squares and byways are now so illuminated that one is never at any point in darkness.

The city is not yet free of fogs, as we learned at the beginning of 1934, but we suffer now none of the sulphurous descents common at the end of last century. Our fuller and wider lighting makes even a black fog penetrable. In the past, if you left your house on a night of fog, to post a letter twenty yards away, you often had a perilous journey back, and were likely, after fifteen minutes, to find yourself far from home. I have been in fogs when one could see nothing a yard ahead, and when bus-drivers and cab-drivers, even when armed with torches and leading their horses, have led them down area-steps or into shop-fronts. Such chaos does not happen to-day in central London. Fog does sometimes paralyse the traffic, but only on the outskirt roads, where lamps are few.

The climate of London, under electrification, has made a change for the better. By our wider streets and our fuller use of glass in place of brick, and our larger and airier buildings, we do not suffer such sticky summers as we once knew, nor such misty winters. We still do not get the full power of sunshine, but our pastel tones seem proper to our streets. They are kind to the eyes, and they give us our cool pulse and comfortable skin. Most of us would not have it otherwise, for it needs only a few days of heat-wave to start us complaining and panting. When the sun retires and the heat-wave breaks, and the streets are grey and violet, we smile and become normal Londoners again.

Another point of change, on which country visitors do not agree with me, is that of noise. The London of to-day is, I maintain, far less noisy than the London of my boyhood. I am constantly being challenged on this, but I stick to it. The *volume* of noise may be greater, but it is less cruel in its effect upon the ear than the old discordant noise. We have a concerted drone in place of random artillery. In those days we had vehicles of all sorts, paving of all sorts, vocal outcries of all sorts, each type making its particular noise in its own key and at its own pitch. Three horse-drays going uphill on cobble-stones, under the vociferous encouragement of their drivers, could make more teeth-grinding and ear-splitting noise than four motor-buses assisted by an electric drill. The motor-buses and the electric drill, by sheer power, cancel each other out, and become as a roll of drums, where the other noise was as of children playing with fire-irons and coal-scuttles. A traffic-block to-day is just a traffic-block. It disentangles itself by the waves of a policeman's hand or a flashing light. Formerly it disentangled itself by forty solo voices yelling forty unrelated recitatives in forty different keys. When two buses or drays locked each other's wheels around the Bank you had turmoil or clamour for some minutes.

Those were the days of self-expression by voice and gesture. Bus-conductors shouted the destinations of their buses; the drivers, when they were not urging other drivers with loud "Ire-ups," abetted them with voice and cracking whip. Newsboys shouted the news. Pedlars shouted their wares. Strident whistles were used for calling cabs. Errand-boys whistled and tried to pierce through each other's whistles with that nerve-rending whistle on two fingers. Carts and buses had iron-bound wheels; you could hear them coming two minutes before they reached you. Throughout the day the larger streets gave out an intermittent racket. To-day they give out a constant grinding hum, through which the changing of gears can scarcely be perceived. After midnight, London is certainly, without argument, quieter than it was. No whistling for cabs; scarcely ever a drunken quarrel, and then only a quiet one; no roaring boys in dishevelled evening clothes, save on Boat Race nights; and little work for the police. In this petrol and electricity age, the centre of London is quickly cleared at night, and though the "three o'clock in the morning boys" still exist they do not trouble central London. They make their whoopee at night-clubs and road-houses twenty and thirty miles out.

One reflection of the conquering motor is the closing to passengers of many London railway stations. Among those which have gone in the last twenty-five years are Grosvenor Road, Walworth Road, Spa Road, Borough Road, Southwark Park. The motor-bus and the Tube, which penetrate and extend to regions untouched by the old horse-buses, have rendered them unnecessary. In addition, there is the general movement outwards. Workers need not now live in the near suburbs; the vast development of little towns of small-priced houses in the far suburbs, and the increased activity of the building societies, enable them to live if not in the country at least on the edge of it. That edge is, of course, much farther from the centre than it was in recent times. I have before me a map of London and environs of 1912, which shows many a green space around Willesden, Lee, Mitcham, Wanstead and Finchley. You cannot find those green spaces now; it is difficult even to locate their site. Main roads, which once were lined with hedges and ran through open country, are now built up with shops and residences, and the once-open country is a populous suburb with a name of its own. Shops and houses are with you almost to Uxbridge, Croydon, Slough, Cheshunt, Romford, Dartford and Orpington. Even farther afield, where the current maps show green spaces, they are not really open country spaces. They are pitted and pocked all over with factories, institutions, warehouses, "works," and incipient building operations. Travelling by road to-day you must travel at least thirty miles before you have shaken off the fact and the rumour of London.

Still, however much the fastidious may deplore the scarring of the countryside, and the cheap bungalow and the "ribbon" villages, it must be recognised that this outward thrust has done a great deal towards the clearance of the inner slums. The late nineteenth century made a tentative effort towards dealing with the problem, but one could hardly call it successful. In place of decayed, but rather picturesque, hovels, it gave London those gaunt Bolshevik-looking barracks known as tenements or dwellings. Apart from being a good deal uglier than the original slums, they did nothing to solve the problem. They merely perpetuated it in another form. They merely replaced over-crowded alleys with over-crowded boxes. They took away the lateral slums and created a series of vertical slums, which, even if they were not worse, *looked* worse. The later development of Council estates on the outskirts was a much more sensible idea, and though it has had to meet some criticism, chiefly on the point of the want of social amenities, it will no doubt in time, by combining with the satellite towns and industries, prove to be a solution of the problem. We are seeing all these new urban-rural estates in their transitional, settling-down stage, a stage at which everybody and everything is open to criticism; and we cannot yet perceive what they are going to be. When the years have matured them and made them part of the future English scene we may find that they sink aptly into that new scene.

This sweeping expansion of London into the fields, within the last thirty years, while it has made some once-green suburbs wholly urban, has operated so irrationally that it has missed many a corner, and left bits of the country crystallised in a rocky surrounding of town. Again, a new traffic route, or a by-pass, turns a once-urban district back to its old sequestered green. A few days' wandering around the suburbs reveals many of these incongruities. While some, in these thirty years, have so changed as almost to have shed their old selves, others remain almost as they were, save for the addition of a movie-palace or a tea-shop.

Living in a constantly-changing London, with the ever-present sense of impermanence, there is something of the terrible in coming, as one may, upon some corner familiar to one's childhood, and never seen since, and finding it just as one left it. This has happened once or twice to me, and on each occasion I have had to fly from the spot. Why, I don't know, unless it is fear of meeting oneself, or fear of what London is going to do next. In a hoary cathedral town, or some little place on the Cotswolds or the Cleveland Hills, such a discovery of an unchanged spot gives no surprise to the returned wanderer; but in London it is uncanny. To see the baker's shop, the sweetstuff shop, the ironmonger's shop, just as you left them, with the same names over their doors; the house with the stone portico and the Modes et Robes with the worn red-brick steps unchanged after forty years of London movement, is to suffer a rupture of the time-sense, if not a doubt of the very existence of time and of the reality of one's present self. Almost one expects to see oneself in knickerbockers coming out of the sweetstuff shop, and one's sweetheart, now forty-two, come skipping out of the toy-shop. Or one sees them as goblin shops, living on when long dead in the frozen animation of a spell put upon them on the day one last saw them. To look back upon the past is interesting, if not always pleasing. To walk through this fermenting London, and come suddenly upon the very physical structure and fixtures of the past is frightening. Yet, as I say, it is still possible, and I have had the experience at Ealing, Dulwich and Clapham.

A few weeks ago I went to see whether there was still a spot of London called Dulwich Village. I did not expect to find anything of "village," and I doubted whether even the name survived. But I found that not only the name but the village atmosphere survived. There it was, still a village, and with all the "points" I had known thirty years ago. No trams, no buses, no movies; but red-roofed cottages, front gardens, church, a penthouse shop or two, and a few Georgian mansions. And not far from it an old toll-gate, still taking toll of vehicles. Just a village, as mellow and picturesque as one would find in the rural distances of Surrey or Kent; and ten minutes from Victoria. Yet a near neighbour, Streatham, has so changed in the same period that scarcely any of its topographical points could be identified by one of its returning sons.

After my Dulwich experience I had the contrary experience at Eltham. I had last seen Dulwich thirty years ago, and found it the same. I had last seen Eltham only twenty years ago, and I could not find it. In my time London had not reached it. London then ended at Lee Green, and one got to Eltham and Well Hall either along hedge-bordered roads or across corn fields. On this visit I was aware that we had passed Lewisham, but was not aware when we had passed Lee Green. We were still on tram lines and among houses. I was waiting for Lee Green. Then my friend who was driving me stopped at a cross-roads amid a cluster of shops, and said This was Eltham. I told him he must have made a mistake, and taken the wrong road at Lee. He assured me he hadn't, and produced his map. He then indicated the church, which seemed faintly familiar, but in the wrong place. It was like one of those dreams in which you are in London and the Lake district at the same time, or crossing the Channel in St. Paul's Cathedral, or dining in a restaurant and fighting wolves in Siberia between the soup and the fish. I strongly combated his statement that this was Eltham; I could not link what I saw with what I had known. He got out and asked me to look round the churchyard, and he showed me the memorial of "Seton Merriman" and of other of its prominent sons. I knew then that this was Eltham, but I could see very little of the Eltham I had known, beyond the names of the roads and streets. All the old topographical features were gone, or hidden in a busy little suburb of shopping-streets, tea-shops, movie-palaces, trams, buses, and massed houses. Similar change has visited Elstree. This, up to the time of the war, was a peaceful little village, whose peace in its long life had only once been convulsed. That was when Thurtell and his friends committed their horrid crime upon William Weare:

> They cut his throat from ear to ear,
> His brains they battered in.

To-day its name is "on the map," and it is convulsed every hour by traffic more portentous than the midnight gallop of Mr. Thurtell's gig.

Some of the near suburbs have suffered much less change than those which were, thirty years ago, on the edge. Those districts near the bridges reached their ultimate development in the seventies, and enterprise left them alone and went seeking for other fields. There are corners of Clapham, for example, which are to-day as I knew them in childhood; the Old Town, and The Pavement and The Triangle; and Carpenter's, the confectioners, still display each Christmas their gigantic cake, which was one of the Christmas sights of Clapham in my youngest childhood. Highgate Village, and its Grove and Pond Square are little changed. The Borough High Street has moved scarcely at all from my earliest recollection of it; it is still a dishevelled thoroughfare of miscellaneous shops, warehouses, and old inn-yards serving as railway receiving offices. And Drury Lane, though in the fastnesses of central London, has known little development, save at the Strand end. While Kensington High Street would be almost unrecognisable by one who last saw it in Jubilee year, Notting Hill has scarcely changed its face, and all the difference that Adam Wayne, its Napoleon, would note is an increase of traffic. East Croydon Junction is now an urban station, almost as busy as Clapham Junction. Yet much nearer to London you may find a little wayside station, sunk in a dell, gay with flowers and rockery, with fields on either side of it, and only the spire of a village church, rising above it, to suggest a human settlement. The station is Sydenham Hill, twelve minutes from Victoria. Its clock still bears the initials of the London, Chatham and Dover Railway.

That Clapham should have so many remains of its past is no puzzle, since it was for many years after its early growth a district of large houses kept by well-to-do people of the conservative sort. This helped to maintain its original rural atmosphere and to protect it, in the eighties and nineties, from the "development" of large houses and grounds into twenty little houses, which was going on in suburbs around it and farther out. Those large houses, notable those of Clapham Park and of

North Side and South Side of the Common, had also large gardens, which were among the earliest gardens I knew. Some of them even had meadows and cows, and thirty-five years ago I often became sunburnt in those meadows while helping with the hay-making. Tram-cars, buses, and the "electric railway" were running five minutes away, but once you had passed through the fronts of those houses you were, in a sense, "in the country."

A certain South Side garden was a constant factor of my childhood. It was a proper garden; that is, an assembly of gardens: rose-walk, orangery, vinery, shrubbery, kitchen-garden, hot-house, wall-garden, rock-garden, orchard and paddock, and cedared lawns. There were wonderful children's teas on those lawns; strawberries and cream, the strawberries picked by oneself from the beds; cherries and mulberries from the trees; and unsurpassed cakes made by a queen of cooks. And after tea one raided the currant bushes, or played Spies in the shrubbery, or Hot Rice in the paddock. Just outside were newsboys with the four-thirty winner, ice-cream stalls, penny bazaars, Home and Colonial stores, and all the fixtures of town; but the evening sun falling across those lawns and paddock, and the thrushes in the pear-tree and the rooks in the elms, suffused it with the feeling of a garden in the deep shires.

By my own observation, and vicariously, through the talk of parents and grandparents, I have a hundred years' memories of Clapham, and it seemed to me then that the

Clapham of those old houses and gardens was outside the time-action which was tinging all the rest of that suburb. It was, I felt, my grandfather's Clapham, preserved behind the modern High Street by some alchemy of his, so that he could show it to me. To some extent it was, for amid all the bustle of a main-road suburb one was constantly meeting, as one can meet to-day, isolated patches of the hamlet atmosphere. Side by side with the tram-cars you could then see "the squire of Clapham" (Mr. Thornton, I think), riding horse-back round the Old Town; and the cottage to which my grandfather took his bride was still in occupation and unaffected by the "electric railway" or any other progress. Within two minutes of the High Street was a farmyard (Denny's) from which children, as though in the heart of the country, fetched milk in the afternoons; and off the streets of little villas one could find an occasional hedgerowed lane leading to another street of little villas.

Most of the old houses and their gardens had been built and tended by three generations, and some of the names of Clapham families of my day are to be found in a directory for the "Environs of London" of 1780. It was that kind of place. People came to it and stayed, and their sons stayed, and *their* sons stayed. In a smaller way it still is that kind of place, for it is one of those suburbs where I see over the shops the same names that were over them in the year of Diamond Jubilee. But while many of its topographical features remain as they were, ignored by development, and the Triangle and the Pentagon and Wren's houses are still there, my garden is not. About

1909 the heirs of the old families took advantage of the car and sought the real country, leaving their large houses unwanted by a labour-saving age. Some of them, on either side of the Common, remain as family houses, but numbers of them were re-constructed and some of them pulled down. That garden which means to me all gardens is now buried under a block of mansion-flats.

A certain part of Ealing, modern as most of it is, shares with Clapham, Wandsworth, and Dulwich, a survival power against the horns of progress, and the little corner where my Aunt Sara lived still looks much as when she saw it. The fields are gone--in Jubilee Year it was really in the country--but the general surroundings keep their old tone. At least once a year I went to "stay" with Aunt Sara, and I can identify now some of the shops where pennies and threepences were spent, notably the Shop of the Super-Excellent Doughnut. I have never eaten doughnuts since my Ealing days; they may still, for all I know, be only a penny each, but I would have to pay a far higher price than that for my doughnut-joy. It is distracting to recall that in those days of clear air I could play with four in a morning, and then eat a mid-day dinner. The sweets shop, which sold penny prize-packets of a more ornate kind than those sold in Clapham, I also found, and the church with its lych-gate, and the ironmonger's shop where I bought my first fret-saws.

When I first knew that corner of Ealing, the District Railway was already running to it; yet it was still country. Behind Aunt Sara's house all was open fields and brooks.

Just across those fields was a large house at which I always looked with respect, as most boys of those years would have done. It was the home of a hero; the home of the monarch of the tight-rope: Blondin. Wandering around it one morning (trespassing, I suppose) I had the honour of seeing and speaking with His Greatness himself, and the further honour of being invited to a glass of milk and a cake at his own kitchen door. That house is now gone, and the fields in which it stood. They have been "developed," and while the little urban corners of that part of Ealing remain as I knew them, the fields are streets of little houses.

These new little houses of the outer ring are a surprising advance on the little houses once considered the standard for small incomes. In this matter, too, things that forty years ago were only to be had by the well-to-do are now part of the everyday of Mr. and Mrs. Everyman. On almost all the new "estates," one finds these little concrete and glass houses fitted with garage, or space for garage; and the kitchen fitted with constant hot water and the latest kitchen gadgets; the bathroom with mirror, towel-rails, wash-basin, oxydised taps, and often a shower; the bedrooms with gas-fires and wardrobes, and the dining-room with oak panelling. Many of the latest have roof sun-parlours, and an all-electric basis. Gas and electric light are so obvious that they are not mentioned. Yet in inner London whole streets may be found where electric light is unknown, and in my youth there were many streets where even gas was unknown. The people in those streets spent their evenings with lamp and candle light, and all cooking throughout the year had to be done by coal fire. The houses were just boxes. Bath-rooms were unknown and fittings other than fireplaces and a cupboard or two, were unthought of. What is commonplace today, such as picture-rails, hot and cold water upstairs, tiled kitchens, etc., belonged then to luxury standards. To-day, indeed, Mr. and Mrs. Everyman enjoy so much comfort that the real "luxury" flats of the expensive districts have a hard job to keep ahead of them.

But there is one point of these new suburban houses, and even of the mansion flats of the better sort, which is not wholly satisfactory. That is the size of the rooms. A few years ago it was announced that, under a planning scheme for London, certain tracts of Victorian London were to be preserved. I wondered why. I felt that with the Houses of Parliament, Shaftesbury Avenue, Bayswater Road, Northumberland Avenue, and a few other treasures, we had all the relics of that period we could need, and that the disappearance of the stucco villas around Regent's Park would be no loss. Each age has the architecture that suits it, and it is only rarely that the architecture of one age delights other ages. The Tudor and early Georgian architects produced towns and streets that have satisfied many generations, but Victorian work was for Victorians. Uncomely building came in with industrialism, about the time of the Regency, and lasted over one hundred years. You may see it in being all over London, and when you see it you may wonder as I did what there is about it to merit preservation.

Now that industry, through mechanisation, has begun to shed much of its ugliness, we are beginning to find beauty again, and I can imagine antiquarian folk of 2034 protesting against the vandalism of pulling down those charming little pieces of the early twentieth century--Shell-Mex House and Broadcasting House. I could not, at the time, see any vandalism in pulling down the Victorian streets, whether they were in Kensington or in Kennington, and I thought for half an hour before I could see any reason in preserving them. The reason, of course, has nothing to do with æsthetic. It lies, if my fancy is right, in that very solidity we used to despise, but which those who live in modern flats are beginning to reconsider. It is still certain that the Victorians knew little about beauty. It is fairly certain that they knew nothing about convenience. It is not so certain that they did not know something about making homes.

They did at least know what a *room* was, and they did not take the rabbit-hutch as their standard. When they gave you a dining-room they gave you a dining-room, not a cupboard into which a table and six chairs and a Jacobean dresser just fit. When they gave you a kitchen, they gave you a kitchen; not a couple of telephone-boxes, but a room in which three cooks would spoil the broth without colliding. They did not, naturally, offer any labour-saving facilities, since in their time there was no occasion for saving labour. Money had such value that servants could be had for ten, twelve, fourteen pounds a year, and could be happy on it. Few people to-day have sufficient means to keep up those houses, which require four or five servants at much higher wages than fourteen pounds. But, split up into flats, they make a good object-lesson for our modern flat-designers. In small portions they are just as easy to run as the labour-saving rabbit-hutches, and what they lack in convenience is compensated by the larger personal radius they offer.

I happen to live in a part of one of these Victorian homes, and have found that it has its qualities. It has not the latest American conveniences and none of the elegance of the Queen Anne period. But it has points not to be found in the newest examples of home-building. Friends of mine, who used to pity me and tell me of the snappy little gadgets fitted in their up-to-date flats, have begun to remark on the size of my rooms; on the fact that they can take a walk in them. In their own flats they can take five steps from the drawing-room and reach the bedroom; and four steps from the bathroom brings them to the breakfast-table. The size of their kitchinette absolves them from giving dinners to their friends at home, and enables them to entertain in restaurants at seven times the cost of entertaining at home. In my Victorian flat the drawing-room would permit twelve couples to waltz without collision, even if their waltzing was of the standard of the parish hall. To reach the front door from my study means a journey of eighteen paces, and the hall is long and wide enough for a game of badminton.

Clearly there is a case for preserving these Victorian houses, since two friends of mine, who are paying three times my rent for modern rabbit-hutches, have asked me to let them know if I think of giving up my flat. These houses have little claim to preservation as historical pieces, but they could, if preserved, be of some service. Classes of young architects, who will be designing our children's villas and flats, might be driven out to them once a week, and shown practical illustrations of what a "room" should be. Labour-saving was an excellent and necessary development, but I cannot understand why the architect should have said in his heart: "I am saving you labour. Therefore you must have smaller rooms." It seems tautology.

But these new little houses on the extra-suburban estates have had a good effect on London and on the people's condition and spirits. Poverty, as I said earlier, still smudges the city, but it is not so dense black as it was, and it is centred mainly on lack of work, not, as formerly, on wretched wages. There is better distribution of amenities and a higher tone in the living of all classes. Even in the poorest alleys you no longer see children clad in ungainly assortments of their parents' clothes. Today, however shabby they may be, they wear their own clothes. You no longer see barefoot waifs begging in the streets. They still beg, but they make a sport of it, as with grottoes, or with painted faces and fancy dress a fortnight before Guy Fawkes Day. If you do, in the summer, see children scampering about without shoes or stockings it is due to their delight in modern hygiene, not to social misery. Even outside the Labour Exchanges and Night Shelters, and in the processions of Hunger Marchers, you do not see men in the utter rags that were common at the end of last century. They are not sufficiently clad, but they are outwardly decent. The poverty that is still with us--and dire poverty it is--is a silent and invisible poverty, and therefore perhaps more potent in its after-effects, which the next generation will be meeting. It is a poverty, not of rags and beggars, but of under-nourishment, of unoccupied minds, of daily frustrated hopes, of fruitless endeavour, of the gradual seeding of moral quality and independence. It is a poverty of which the general public gets only a flashing revelation when some despairing creature, hitherto respectable, is driven to petty offences.

As this poverty is invisible, so is its opposite of great wealth. The car made the first bite towards the decay of displayed equipage and strings of footmen. The war was another factor, in that it made display indecent. With the coming of the post-war days people had got used to the easier and simpler life of war-time, and had no desire to return to display. The service-flat attracted many people from the trials and troubles of keeping up large town houses, and the younger people among the rich preferred to forsake the solidity of the parental home for the adventure of studio life and camps in the haylofts of mews. Families used to live in their homes. To-day they only lodge in their homes, and live out. Even where establishments are kept up, they are kept up with a minimum of formality and style. Public ostentation requires leisure for the doing and for the result. To make its effect it must have people to look on. To-day nobody has time to look on at a pageant or to produce one. Liveries are plainer; domestics are fewer; social occasions are speedier. It is difficult now to guess from outward evidence who is wealthy and who is not. The woman who gives a reception in a mansion of one of the statelier squares may have merely hired it and an outside staff for the night. The man riding in the bus or the Tube may be wealthier than the man in the Rolls-Royce. In the fashionable restaurants of the St. James district you may see any evening really wealthy people, quite hard-up people, and people who are neither, all looking alike.

Wealth is about, but it does not flaunt itself in public. The streets of London are no longer a melodrama of St. Giles and St. James. St. Giles strolls about St. James, and sits in tea-shops at the corner of streets where rents are eight-hundred a year; and the male residents of those streets stroll about in clothes which seem expressly designed to make them indistinguishable from the three-pound-ten St. Giles. From casual observation a foreigner might assume, and be justified in assuming, that London was a city whose people had all about the same level of income. Appearances convey nothing to-day, except to credulous West End shopmen and hotel-keepers, and to those whose greed makes them the victims of confidence men.

All streets are everyman's streets. The East End is as quiet and respectable as any other quarter; the lower reaches of the river are perhaps safer for the innocent than Shaftesbury Avenue; and crime has no longer any definite headquarters, nor is it limited to any definite class. The last battle fought on London's soil--the battle of Sidney Street--put the finishing touch to the East End as a crime-centre. Lawlessness now breaks out anywhere, but, like wealth, it operates with as little fuss as possible. The police-whistle is heard in the streets much less frequently than at any time in my recollection, and a street-fight in any quarter is a rare event.

The modern streets of London, deficient as they may be in melodrama, are none the less as rich in interest as they ever were, and while millions of human creatures keep them in being they will continue to be so. From my earliest years they have been my hobby. Before I was in my teens I loved, when possible, to roam about them alone. I was not then allowed or able to get far, but later, from fifteen onwards, I spent my evenings in lonely wanderings. I went about and got muzzy with London, swallowing every second so many thrilling impressions that I could digest none of them. One wanders now at night through a London of brilliance; only here and there does one find a gorge of darkness, and then it is only violet darkness. One wandered in those days through a London of sombre magnificence, its black darkness shot with gleams and twinkles. It was the London which Whistler saw, a London of low tones and melting shades. Under to-day's wide and intense lighting, the thousand and one lovely nocturnes which then presented themselves each night have been dissolved, and he would have to search in distant alleys to find his silver and lilac tints.

I found many of them on those wanderings, and encountered many little episodes which remain with me to this day when important public spectacles have passed from memory. When I sit still and recall those wanderings I recall none of the big scenes through which I passed nor any of the moments which at the time were profound. I recall only trifles which at the time I did not consciously notice. Why these things stick, and, without mental guidance, paint themselves on the mind when it is empty, I cannot say; but when brooding on London I find myself seeing things of this sort--

A voluble market-woman in a horse-bus of thirty years ago, describing to an aloof and embarrassed passenger the perfect way of cooking bloaters.

A Sunday morning in South London--one of hundreds which by some trick has isolated itself. Deserted street. Blind shops. Refuse in gutter. Dust blowing in clouds. The whole scene set to music by the miserable bells of four churches wrangling against each other.

Portland Place in the dim past. Langham Hotel. Hansom cabs. Broughams. Cockaded footmen. Milk-women. A voice from an open doorway: "Tell them I'll be dining at the club."

Wooden stands for the Coronation show in Borough High Street. Workmen testing their stability by jumping on them at the word of command.

The smell of the original Underground Railway.

Midnight in Caledonian Road. A woman crossing the road; a man standing at a corner under a lamp; a cat in a doorway; a poster, half-torn from the hoarding, flapping in the breeze.

A waiter doing up his bootlace at the door of an Italian restaurant in Soho.

Young girl and schoolboy kissing in a dark doorway of Church Street, Notting Hill.

The crowd under the clock at Charing Cross station one winter night. A girl in a blue dress; a porter stroking his face; an old lady with a dog; a young man in brown overcoat reading a newspaper.

October evening in a street of Bloomsbury. The street powder-blue. The two lamps making sick gasps. The glow of a roast-chestnut stall. A solitary policeman funeral-marching.

Cornhill at one in the morning. Not a creature or vehicle in sight. A full moon. A breathlessness in the air. The buildings rapt and watchful, as though waiting for some portentous event. And then somebody whistling.

Why this stuff thrusts itself forward and ousts more serious things, is a question which only the Vienna school, I suppose, could answer. Though, looking over my Caledonian Market of memories, I doubt if even they could make much of it. The only use I can see in it is that of a working scenario for a plotless novel.

The new aspects and vistas disclosed by modern lighting have their own quality. London at night is no longer lapped in sullen brooding. It shines. It is a proud and burnished London, dressed for social life. Throughout its centre it offers white avenues, all of light, and elsewhere are caverns and recesses of gold and diamond. Even the roofs, which once met the upper darkness in an invisible smudge, are now defined in sharp relief. Seen from a height, it is a glittering plain, slashed with bands of processional light, which are the main streets; and even the minor byways make their gilded chains. It does not, of course, match Paris or New York, because it is London. However flooded with light it may be, it will still be heavier in tone than those examples of song and yell. Neither its body nor its spirit can throw back light in their exultant fashion. It wears its light rather with grandeur, absorbing it; and while that light may be considered not too lustrous by visitors from European cities, in London it is brilliance. If George R. Sims were writing his *Lights of London* to-day, he would have to intensify his epithets; incidentally, since the lights of London are now met far beyond Highgate, his young people would have a shorter walk. The mystic quality of the old, long-spaced lamplight, which so moved De

Quincey, vanished long ago; and even the much later Richard le Gallienne could not now sing of the iron lilies of the Strand. Peonies or orchids would be the word. Yet now, as always, they are the lights of London. From rush-light and candle-light, through lanthorn and oil and gas, to these days of electricity and flood-lighting, they have had, beyond their purpose of showing the way, the potency to live in the memories of those who have been happy or forlorn among them.

Much of the modern brilliance is due not only to municipal operations but to the advertisers and their night-signs. Some of us feel that they have overdone it, but as advertisers do that with everything, complaint is futile and perhaps, in the circumstances, ungenerous. They have given the evening face of London, if not jewels, at least bright gauds, and have eased that note of grief which used to mark its nocturnal. If, in doing so, they have robbed it of serenity, the young may be trusted to tell us that they miss nothing. When the first night-sign was set up above the heads of Londoners I cannot say. No doubt the advertisers keep some record of the pioneers in that calling whose very essence is pioneering. The earliest that my memory offers is one in Trafalgar Square which advertised Vinolia Soap. I do not think it spelt it letter by letter; that was a later innovation for the vexing of our nerves. I think it was a stationary blaze. I know that we stood and stared at it, even as people from the shires now stand and stare at the coruscating fables of Piccadilly Circus and Leicester Square.

Perhaps the changes that have come over the streets of London in my time are most immediately observed in that stronghold of conservatism and has-been-ism, the City. There they stand out, and wandering about it the other day I had some trouble in finding my way. When I knew it, Crosby Hall was standing where it was built, and in those days it still held many traces of the hard gloom and mouldering dinge in which Dickens presented it. There were still numbers of dens below ground in which ill-paid clerks worked for small firms under all-day artificial light. There were dusty garrets up four pairs of stairs in which six or seven people worked together. Light, in its narrow alleys, was so hard to come by that they tried to trap it by means of sheets of glass projecting from each window. Many of the side-streets, which housed hundreds of offices, were as slummy as a court of King's Cross or Haggerston. The general impression left with me, after the short time I spent there, was of fustiness, superannuated gloom, and cramp; plus, of course, the tight-lipped commercial spirit which took no account of these things so long as it could do business. One quarter of its life in those days, I should imagine, happened underground. Men worked underground, and when they went out to lunch they again went underground. Almost every building had a basement, and it was always in use. On a summer day, one could look down through gratings, and see clerks scribbling in books under electric light.

Wherever one looked the scene was colourless. The buildings had a tone peculiar to the City, for which there is no name. It wasn't black or brown or dun or drab. It was not so definite as the tone of mud or the tone of cobwebs or manure. It was such a tone as you might get from wet smoke mixed with Army-blanket fluff and engine smuts. Every street was riddled with courts and alleys, where this tone was thicker, and each of these courts and alleys was a rabbit warren. In some kinds of business the "living-in" system was in force; the young clerks had a dormitory at the top of the building and a dining-room in the cellar; and, save for a few hours of the evening, they spent their young lives in the City's atmosphere. Nobody thought it anything but a sound system. They never do. It is the hardest job to get any one generation to perceive the distresses of its own time. It can perceive only the distresses of the past, and will talk complacently of how enlightened and progressive *we* are as compared with the last generation, and will regard anybody who points out current short-comings as a sentimental agitator.

Still, the present generation has made a great improvement in the appearance of the City, and in its conditions generally, as against what they were. It has more air, more space, less twilight, and fewer nests of moles and bats. Its nineteenth-century dinge has been replaced by brilliant stone and much glass. Cornhill, Leadenhall Street, Moorgate Street and Gracechurch Street have all responded to the spirit of the age and the new attitude to commerce. In the past it was held that anything pertaining to this trite and shabby matter must be dour and funereal--goodness knows why, unless to hide the trite and shabby reality. To-day, however, business men seem to have realised the truth of huckstering. Business premises now have a musical-comedy touch, and business is conducted almost with nonchalance. Field-marshals at the door, dapper young men within, and almond-paste and frosted-sugar on the front. Business is the new career, the new fun; and the streets have caught this spirit. Even the Bank, the last spot where one would look for change, has put on a Montparnasse head-dress.

In my wanderings about the streets whose stones I once so hated, I had, as I say, some trouble in recognising them. Even after checking their names at the corners, I had to look again to see anything of the street I knew. Leadenhall Street, Lime Street and Fenchurch Street have quite changed their faces, and I recognised Leadenhall Street only from the entrance to its labyrinthine Market, which still makes an incongruity in that world of banks and shipping-offices. Gracechurch Street I walked through and did not know that it was Gracechurch Street until I saw the statue of King William at its end. The "oldest house in London" was gone from Cheapside; also Williamson's Hotel, once the residence of London's Lord Mayors; but Honey Lane Market I found still living, and still, with its little shops, a retail market. The plane-tree of Poor Susan still takes up space which might be used for money-grubbing, and casts its agreeable shade over the corner of Wood Street, and Bow Bells are still there, though at the time of writing the church is under repair. The Royal Exchange is still waiting for somebody to put a glass case over it, and Pimm's is still serving its "No. 1 Cup." Queen Victoria Street and Cannon Street look pretty much as they did, and in a world of change it was reassuring to find Cannon Street Station still lending its comeliness to a somewhat less comely street. But elsewhere, differences met me at every corner. Eastcheap and Pudding Lane were both more trim than when I last saw them, and Billingsgate had shed much of its reek and noise. New Broad Street and London Wall were more imposing, and the approach to London Bridge much brighter. But the Bridge, at nine in the morning and six in the evening, is still one of the major sights of London for those to whom London means something more than museums and fashionable streets. There, at those hours, you have in essence the life of the average man of all time--Going to Work; Returning Home. It is a spectacle of every city of the world to-day, and a modern replica of the spectacle that has punctuated every day of our world since first there were cities and work. It is one of those spectacles which, after you have seen the historical monuments and the great streets and the high features of London, and its major social events, may give you a flash of illumination upon its spirit and bring its secret to life for you.

One missing feature, whose absence I regretted, was a person who, in his day, was known far outside the City boundaries, and came to mind as naturally as Gog and Magog whenever the City was mentioned. I mean that true stalwart of the City, the Lord Mayor's Coachman of the period of the nineteen-noughts. He was always the most impressive and imperturbable figure of the Show, and London reserved a special cheer for him as the procession passed. He was so much a public figure that in those days you could buy picture-postcards of him. Among the too-unpleasantly familiar points for which I looked in vain (and was thereby glad) was one which had some associations not wholly unpleasant. This was the cheap tea-shop where I spent some burning hours in first looking into some new country of the World's Classics or the Camelot reprints. In its place I found a portent of the new times; what in my City days would have been an anomaly in that square mile of the masculine: a shop devoted to perfumes, lip-sticks, face-creams and perms.

With all my wanderings of day and night about London there are still some streets I have not walked through. This sometimes worries me until I remember that not even taxi-drivers know every street within the four-mile radius. I don't believe Mr. Wilfred Whitten does. No man can. Life is not long enough, and the time for wandering is no more ample than the time for standing and staring. Only Mr. W. H. Davies' cows have enough time for this, and only cats have enough time for exploring every by-street. We humans can know only a little of the earth, and we Londoners can know only a little of our London. The born Londoner having the whole giant city to love, is so embarrassed by its richness, that he is compelled to set his affection upon a few spots of it. Those spots become for each of us a crystallisation of all that London means to us. It is seldom that they are chosen from the major tracts of the city; they are scarcely ever guide-book spots. As we do not remember people by their flagrant characteristics, but by their oddities and subtleties, so the Londoner, far from home and thinking of London, does not think of Big Ben or St. Paul's or the Tower Bridge. It is the trifles that stick, and almost always he will think of a lamp-post or a street-refuge; a bus-stop or an Underground station. A friend of mine, who lives in the hard sunshine of California, sees instantly, on hearing the word London, Doulton's tower at Lambeth. For myself, the word flashes to me, before I have time to think, Victoria Street on a wet evening. There may be, here and there, men in whom London evokes only Piccadilly or Bond Street or Pall Mall. But these are men who have never really known London; men to whom London was merely a playground during vacations, and who know only the outstanding bits known to visitors. These bits are no more than the lowest common denominators of London for the lazy and unperceiving mind. This type of mind, at the word Paris sees the Eiffel Tower or Notre Dame or Montmartre; and at the word New York sees sky-scrapers. But these features, prominent as they are, say little about their cities. The whole of Paris may be caught in a letter-box, and the whole of New York in a store-clerk's gesture.

So charged with life is London that its most common attitude, its smallest finger-joint, seems to be its complete expression; and it is here that the true Londoner catches its pulse. I learned from a sailor that whenever he thought of London he saw first the ferry-boats at Woolwich. Another, not a native, but a twenty-years resident, told me that the essence of London for him lived in the first bit of London he saw--Praed Street, Paddington. An American, when I asked him what he saw as the essence of London; what it was that gave him the realisation of being in a foreign city, said--"Pavement artists." Six native Londoners to whom I lately put the question mentioned these points as rising unbidden to their minds at thought of London: The shot-tower at Waterloo Bridge--the "Angel" at Islington--the Battersea Power Station--St. Clement Danes--Holborn Viaduct--the view of Cannon Street Station seen from Southwark. These were, for them, intrinsic London, surpassing in expression any of the picture-postcard features. London in slippers, as it were. It is this London which the stranger ought to see, and seldom does, except when he walks about with me. And then he doesn't like it; behind my back he curses me for showing him such dull stuff when he wanted to see lively features like The Bank and the Mansion House and Nelson's Monument.

But to see the Londoner's London you *must* walk through streets which, to the eye, and to certain kinds of mind, are drab and insipid. Behind this outward drabness and insipidity is the real London. You will find it in Southwark, in Pimlico, in Finsbury; and in Islington, Clerkenwell, Bloomsbury, Lambeth. For these quarters are the womb whence grew the great London of to-day. You might try a walk from Oxford Circus to Theobald's Road, and thence by Clerkenwell Road and Old Street (the first of London's highways) to Shoreditch. On this walk many essential factors of

London are to be seen, but you will probably give it up half-way, and I won't blame you. Essentials are seldom picturesque. If you do make it, and find it interesting, you might care to make others. You might go over Westminster Bridge, turn into Lower Marsh and on to the New Cut, and across Blackfriars Road, and through Union Street to Southwark Bridge Road. Follow this road to Southwark Bridge and Bankside. Explore Bankside, in and out of its courts and alleys. Here is an active bit of London of today linked with the importance of three hundred years ago, as you will note from the street-names: Clink Street, Paris Garden, Bear Garden. If that bores you, wait for a Saturday evening, and from King's Cross ascend Pentonville, and half-way up turn into Penton Street. Take the fourth on the right of this, and you come into Chapel Street--a typical Saturday-night London market. If you want to know something of London life and Londoners, apart from Jermyn Street and Knightsbridge, talk with the stallholders. From Chapel Street you can get into Liverpool Road, which brings you to Upper Street, Islington. Islington has played a large part in London's everyday life since the end of the seventeenth century, and a study of the wide thoroughfare of Upper Street, and its representative life, should teach you a good deal about London. You might then cross the road into the quaint and neglected byway which is the original High Street of Islington. From there you could go north and explore the lost land enclosed by Essex Road (part of the original Great North Road to Scotland), City Road and Kingsland Road; or you could cross the road by the "Angel" and improve your mind at the Sadler's Wells Theatre. If you make these walks without a wholly damped spirit, you might be able to stand the one that follows--though I doubt it. At the south of London Bridge turn into Tooley Street and take Stoney Lane on the left, which brings you into Pickle Herring Street. Follow this into Shad Thames, and follow Shad Thames to Dockhead. Then, by way of Mill Street, to Bermondsey Wall, which leads into Rotherhithe Street, and so to Surrey Commercial Docks and Deptford. This walk is pricked at every step with the spirit, and often the stuff, of history; and, as a makeweight, it is loaded with the voice and the hand of the London which supports the London that everybody knows as London. But you don't know what I'm offering you in that walk. Long before you reach Deptford, you will, I fancy, be looking anxiously for taxis, buses, or even trams.

Really, there is but one way for the stranger to see London in such a way as to know it. That is, by not looking at it. If you go about with carefully studious eyes and a programme of sights to be visited--famous streets, buildings, amusements, galleries, parks--you will learn a good deal about the London that every stranger knows, but you will never catch the heart-beat of London. There is no intensive method of doing this. You catch it by fits and starts in a hundred-and-one unexpected and unconsidered spots; by moving about London as you move about your own city or town, taking it in by casual glances, or even ignoring it. Do not go out to "see" anything or "do" anything. Wander idly about it and let it enter your skin in its own haphazard ways. If you do this, you may leave London without being able to say how many kings are buried in Westminster Abbey, or in which part of the Tower Raleigh was imprisoned; and yet you will have seen more of the essential London than the guide-book student. You may not be able to tell your friends at home which restaurant has the best cabaret, or what is the "right" hotel to patronise, but you will be able to tell them where De Beauvoir Town is, and why; and how you found Freezywater; and how you went to Cyprus. You might be able to tell them more than I can; you might be able to tell them where Fulham Road ends.

Most people, when visiting London, see only a minority aspect of its life. They spend their time in the particular world into which they happened to alight. They see historic London, or architectural London, or fashionable London; literary London or political London; and go away thinking they have seen London. The special is never typical, and whatever is most talked about and clamours for attention should always be suspected as unrepresentative. The typical life of a city is seen not in its best features or its worst; not in its highest or its lowest ranks, or in its coteries. It is seen in the daily moods and phases of its unexpressive streets and its unvocal millions. It is these that give it its rich and abiding spirit, across which the changes of fashion and the play of the minorities merely flit; and it is these that you must see if you would know that city. The best way to do this is to go about by yourself. Lose yourself in London. Take your lunch wherever you happen to be at lunch-time, in any kind of café. Just be in London, doing nothing that you would not do at home, and within a week or so London, the uncelebrated but essential London, will have revealed itself to you.

The man who leaves his companions to be conducted round the Tower, and slips off and wanders about East Smithfield, looking into doorways and windows, will come back with a better collection of Londoniana than they. And if they spend the evening in dining at a cosmopolitan restaurant and sitting in the stalls of a West End theatre, while he goes off and dines with a London friend at the friend's everyday club, and finishes in the circle of a music-hall, he may not have so high a time as they, but he will learn a lot about the backbone-life of London. And when, later, he reads of London in his own papers, it will mean something more to him than Whitehall and famous streets and antiquities. A good way of getting some impression of the London known to its daily millions is to take the first bus you see, and go as far as you may for threepence. Then get another bus and spend another threepence. And so on. Or take one of the circular-route tram-cars from the Embankment, which go to places unheard-of by those who regard London as a square half-mile centred on Piccadilly Circus. Then try a ride at two o'clock in the morning on an all-night bus-route. This will give you a new view of London and an idea of the many worlds that go to make up the superficial worlds. The tour may bore you or depress you; perhaps both; and you will wish yourself back in the centre of things.

But you will have seen the average Londoner's London. No doubt you will never want to see it again, or to have any acquaintance with the average Londoner. And I will grant you some justification. But your tour will not have been wasted. It will have given you, for one thing, some idea of the vast extent of London, which the average visitor never gets. And your experience of the typical London of the millions will have helped you to resolve that unpolished life with the life of political London and intellectual London and fashionable London, and the tradition of historic London; and so lead you to an understanding of London as a living body functioning as one but composed of a hundred incongruous organisms.

If you follow my suggestions of aimless wanderings, you will come upon picturesque or odd corners that are not recorded in even the more esoteric guide-books; and upon many a little encounter and experience. It will be from one of these--the peculiar moment that mates with your peculiar vibrations--that you will get a vision of the soul of London. It may be that London Bridge morning and evening crowd, just mentioned. It may be an old building or a new building. It may be a vista of chimneypots. It may be a restaurant scene. It may be a lonely figure crossing a deserted street. It may be a Sunday crowd in a park. It may be a view from one of the bridges. It may be a chance remark overheard from passers-by. It may be a queer-shaped lamp in a side street. It may be a domestic interior seen through open windows. Whatever it is, it will have more power over you than any of the known and much-celebrated points.

I have tried this method myself in strange cities; in Brussels, in Marseilles, in Paris, Lyons, Antwerp; and always the little thing, the everyday thing which the people of that city never mentioned, was the thing which enabled me to realise that city and isolate it from all others. Do not, therefore, make yourself interested in what you have heard or read about London. Wait until you find something that really stirs you. When you do, you will recognise it as the one thing which, where all the "sights" have failed, has brought London to life for you.

One or two of my suggested rambles will take you over the bridges to a London which few people see unless they happen to be going to Waterloo or the Oval. It has always seemed to me a little unfair that the north bank should have almost all the London that "counts," and that the south side should be a draggle-tailed terra incognita. All that the world means when it says London is to be found on the Strand side, which has seen almost all the official and cultural development of the city. Possibly the marsh-lands on the other side had something to do with this in the beginning, but as they were drained centuries ago one would think that the south might now have a share in recognised London. So far it possesses two features only--important features, though of little interest to the general visitor. It possesses London's seat of Government, the County Hall, and the Church's seat of Government, Lambeth Palace. It is also the real land of Cockaigne, the true home of that spirit which gives the common Londoner his distinctive hue and quiddity. But that fact seems to interest nobody save comic draughtsmen. What it seems to need to bring its territory into London proper is a Changing of the Guard or a Leicester Square. It might then begin to look up. Failing those features, it must jog along unregarded, as it has jogged along for the last century or so. In the past, it was not without attention. It was once the centre of the theatre and amusement world (Bankside), and later it was the resort of fashion (Vauxhall). But since those days it has lived, not as London, but as South London, and I doubt if even the shifting of Charing Cross station to its bank, which has long been talked-of, will restore it to the picture.

That, of course, is looking into the distant future. It is possible that my infant godson may live long enough to see the removal of Charing Cross and the end of its bridge. (To think that that structure took the place of the graceful bridge now at Clifton-on-Avon.) It is possible that he may live to see the completion of a new Waterloo Bridge. When the English have been talking about a necessary action for ten years, and have spent another ten in planning how to carry it out, it is a fair bet that one fine day, within a third decade, they will make a job of it. That is our way, and that is why London has time to grow a patina and to develop character in new streets and new buildings often before they are completed. And by the time some ugly and long-condemned feature actually comes to be demolished, we have grown fond of it and are loth to let it go. It is these bits of ugliness standing alongside the beauties of London that arouse the astonishment of strangers. They wonder why, and none of us can explain. We can only make some limp reference to the illogical English character, which does these things, and then waits for people to ask why. There are our public statues which, like our railway stations, have stood firm against the spirit of dignity and amenity that has affected most other aspects of London through this century. Our commercial men have been more alert than the public authorities, and such good statuary as London has is due to them. They have been sensible of the times; but while their buildings are adorned by the work of Jacob Epstein and Eric Gill, the public statues of the great remain as banal as they always were. With two such spaces as Parliament Square and Trafalgar Square offering perfect sites for beautiful statuary, the best we can do with them is to fill them with Madame Tussaud effigies. Foreigners look at them and then look blandly elsewhere, as they would if served with a dusty plate at an elegant table.

On the question of South London, many foreigners have asked me why the map of London shows it as a city divided by a river, when in fact the vast tract on the south bank has no part in it, and the river is really its boundary. I have been able to give them no answer save that it's just happened like that, and nobody has bothered about it. The streets of London, for all allusive purposes, are those on the north bank. The streets on the other side are merely streets in Lambeth and Southwark.

There are none to-day in the remotest hamlets so credulous as to think of the streets of London as paved with gold, or even of a London rich in opportunity. Yet still those streets are the magnet for all that counts in England. The provinces may hold themselves of more importance; Manchester, Birmingham, Newcastle and Leeds may have scant regard for the metropolis, and see it only as a clearing-house for their thought and their action. But the desire of nine Englishmen in ten is to reach London and London's approval. All who are outstanding in art, literature, science, music, medicine, law and the other intelligent departments of life, come sooner or later to London. And few provincials come to it who are not caught and held by it, and, after all their early criticism, do not find it and its life superior to life in Bradford, Huddersfield, Leicester, Nottingham, or even Manchester. Often those who want to go back find themselves staying on year by year, unable to leave it. They have found that it is a city affording little opportunity to the seeker; a city of closed doors; a city where fortunes may be spent and very seldom made; a city that remains indifferent to industry and enterprise; a city that has broken more hearts than it has rejoiced. And still they would rather be poor in London than rich in Huddersfield. Without making the smallest effort to placate them or hold them, it has got them for the rest of their lives. And it will continue to get them, for without them it could not be London.

No matter how often or how violently it changes its face and its dress, its mighty heart remains unchanged. The making of history does not tire it. The longer its story becomes, the more vigorously does it pulse and move, since it draws upon the young blood and ardent fancy of every generation. It is fed and coloured not by the people of any one part of England, but by people from the streets and pastures of every county. From Lydgate's London, through Chaucer's, Dekker's, Ben Jonson's, Addison's, Dr. Johnson's, Lamb's, Dickens' and H. G. Wells' Londons, it remains constantly the expression of the soul and temper of the nation. From time to time, the elderly, faced with change, foresee the end of London, forgetting that what they are foreseeing is merely the end of their own idea of London. Many expressions of this attitude occur in literature; premature elegies on its passing. There is Maginn, with his lament on the destruction entailed by the making of Trafalgar Square:

> Oh, London won't be London long,
> For 'twill be all pulled down;
> And I shall sing a funeral song
> O'er that time-honoured town.

A bad miss, that first line. Almost all the London that Maginn knew *has* been pulled down, and London is still London. It has been a thousand personalities to successive generations, and it has survived all their ideas of it, as it will survive ours. It may in time come to such an end as that of the once-important Cinque Ports, but it is scarcely likely to reach that end in this century. If the adult eyes of to-day could see it in the year 2000, they would doubtless find little to remind them of the London they knew; but for the people going about it, it will mean everything that our London means to us. It will be then, as always, the crystallisation of the contemporary spirit of the English.

www.ingramcontent.com/pod-product-compliance
Lightning Source LLC
Chambersburg PA
CBHW021701240426
R18188600001B/R181886PG43670CBX00001B/1